The Journal of Andrew Fuller Studies

Published in the United States of America
by The Andrew Fuller Center for Baptist Studies
The Southern Baptist Theological Seminary
2825 Lexington Road
Louisville, Kentucky 40280

© The Andrew Fuller Center for Baptist Studies 2025

All rights reserved. No part of this publication may be reproduced, stored in a retrieval system, or transmitted, in any form or by any means, without the prior permission in writing of The Andrew Fuller Center for Baptist Studies, or as expressly permitted by law, by license, or under terms agreed with the appropriate reproduction rights organization.

ISBN 978-1-77484-164-8

Printed by H&E Publishing, Peterborough, Ontario, Canada

The Journal of Andrew Fuller Studies

The Journal of Andrew Fuller Studies is an open access, double-blind peer-reviewed, scholarly journal published online biannually in February and September by the Andrew Fuller Center for Baptist Studies (under the auspices of The Southern Baptist Theological Seminary). The publication language of the journal is English. Articles that deal with the life, ministry, and thought of the Baptist pastor-theologian Andrew Fuller are very welcome, as well as essays on his friends, his Particular Baptist community in the long eighteenth century (1680s–1830s), and the global impact of his thought, known as "Fullerism."

Articles and book reviews are to follow generally the style of Kate L. Turabian, A Manual for Writers of Research Papers, Theses, and Dissertations, 9th ed. (Chicago: University of Chicago Press, 2018). They may be submitted in British, American, Australian, New Zealand, or Canadian English. Articles should be between 5,000 and 8,000 words, excluding footnotes. Articles are to be sent to the Editor and book reviews to the Book Review Editors.

Editor:
Michael A G Haykin, ThD, FRHistS
Chair & Professor of Church History
& Director, The Andrew Fuller Center for Baptist Studies
The Southern Baptist Theological Seminary, Louisville, Kentucky
mhaykin@sbts.edu

Associate editor:
Baiyu Andrew Song, PhD cand.
Assistant Professor of General Education Studies
Heritage College and Seminary
Cambridge, Ontario
bsong@heritagecs.edu

Design editor:
Caleb Anthony Neel, PhD cand.
The Southern Baptist Theological Seminary, Louisville, Kentucky
cneel@sbts.edu

Book review editor:
Caleb Anthony Neel, PhD cand.
The Southern Baptist Theological Seminary, Louisville, Kentucky
cneel@sbts.edu

Editorial board:
Cindy Aalders, DPhil
Director of the John Richard Allison Library
& Assistant Professor of the History of Christianity
Regent College, Vancouver

Dustin B. Bruce, PhD
Dean & Assistant Professor of Christian Theology and Church History
Boyce College
Louisville, Kentucky

Chris W. Crocker, PhD
Pastor, Markdale Baptist Church, ON
& Associate Professor of Church History
Toronto Baptist Seminary
Toronto, Ontario

Chris Chun, PhD
Professor of Church History & Director of the Jonathan Edwards Center
Gateway Seminary
Ontario, California

Jenny-Lyn de Klerk, PhD
Editor, Book Division
Crossway
Wheaton, Illinois

Jason G. Duesing, PhD
Provost & Professor of Historical Theology
Midwestern Baptist Theological Seminary
Kansas City, Missouri

Nathan A. Finn, PhD
Provost & Dean of the University Faculty
North Greenville University
Tigerville, South Carolina

C. Ryan Griffith, PhD
Pastor, Cities Church
St. Paul, Minnesota

Peter J. Morden, PhD
Senior Pastor/Team Leader, Cornerstone Baptist Church
Leeds, England
& Distinguished Visiting Scholar
Spurgeon's College
London, England

Adriaan C. Neele, PhD
Director, Doctoral Program & Professor of Historical Theology
Puritan Reformed Theological Seminary
Grand Rapids, Michigan
& Research Scholar
Yale University, Jonathan Edwards Center
New Haven, Connecticut

Robert Strivens, PhD
Pastor, Bradford on Avon Baptist Church (UK)
& Lecturer in Church History
London Seminary
London, England

Tom Nettles, PhD
Senior Professor of Historical Theology
The Southern Baptist Theological Seminary
Louisville, Kentucky

Blair Waddell, PhD
Pastor, Providence Baptist Church
Huntsville, Alabama

Contents

The Journal of Andrew Fuller Studies
No. 10 Fall 2025

Editorial
Michael A.G. Haykin — 10

Articles
A Reformed voice for divine discourse: An analysis of current debates on prosopological exegesis and the possibility of John Gill (1697–1771) as a fruitful interlocutor — 12
Caleb Hawkins

A devoted husband and sympathetic friend: The life and spirituality of Philip Doddridge — 29
Zeyuan David Zhou

Pastoral usefulness: retrieving wisdom from the letters of Benjamin Beddome — 40
Yuta Seki

A review article of David Mark Rathel, *Andrew Fuller and the Search for a Faith Worthy of All Acceptation* (2024) — 54
Pieter Rouwendal

Texts & documents
A newly discovered letter by Joseph Kinghorn (1766–1832) — 68
Transcribed by Daniel Reed
Annotated and introduced by Baiyu Andrew Song

Book Reviews — 78

Editorial

Michael A.G. Haykin

Michael A.G. Haykin is Chair and Professor of Church History and Director, The Andrew Fuller Center for Baptist Studies at The Southern Baptist Theological Seminary, Louisville, KY.

This year has proven to be a very hectic one for the Editor, and thus the decision was made not to publish an issue of The Journal of Andrew Fuller Studies in the Spring, but to have the next issue, this one, appear in the Fall of 2025. Going forward, we still hope and expect to publish two issues per year.

Our essays in this issue range over a number of subjects that relate to the world of eighteenth-century British Dissent. Caleb Hawkins explores a key element in John Gill's habitus in speaking about God, while Zeyuan David Zhou discusses two key aspects of the piety of Philip Doddridge, namely, marriage and friendship. I have long considered Doddridge to be one of the most attractive figures of his day, and I wish he were better known. Hopefully, this article on Doddridge might prove to be a step in that direction.

Yuta Seki's article, which is drawn from a book that he has recently written on Benjamin Beddome's pastoral theology and that is being published by Wipf and Stock, examines an aspect of pastoral ministry that is quite foreign to much of today's world of pastoralia. In the eighteenth century, when a pastor considered the possibility of accepting a call from another congregation, his congregation first had to be asked if they were willing to "release" their pastor and allow him to consider the call. Personally, I think this a better arrangement than our current practice in which the congregation is usually the last to find out that their pastor is leaving.

Our final article is a review by Pieter Rouwendal of David Rathel's important study, *Andrew Fuller and the Search for a Faith Worthy of All Acceptation* (T&T Clark, 2024). Dr. Rathel's work is significant in that it provides further foundations for the study of Fuller and his response to the so-called Modern Question (namely, should the gospel be freely offered to all and sundry?) of the eighteenth century. Prof Rouwendal does not dispute the importance of Fuller's positive answer to the question, but he does pose some important questions about Rathel's discussion of the background to Fuller's famous *The Gospel Worthy of All Acceptation*. Personally, I am thrilled to see this weighty historical discussion regarding Fuller and his books.

A transcription of a letter by Jospeh Kinghorn by Daniel Reed and annotated by the Associate Editor and some book reviews round out this Fall issue. Enjoy!

A Reformed voice for divine discourse: An analysis of current debates on prosopological exegesis and the possibility of John Gill (1697–1771) as a fruitful interlocutor

Caleb Hawkins

Caleb Hawkins is a pastor at Generations Church in Norcross, GA, who also serves as the managing editor for Hanover Press.

Interpretive conclusions of scripture are often directed by the questions posed to it. In the gospel of Mark, Jesus sees this link by presenting his audience with what he insinuates as an exegetical dilemma in Ps 110:1. Jesus' question in Mark 12:35–37 demands an interpretive decision. If the person of David does not fit the dialogue, then who does? Jesus is subtly illuminating himself as the natural character for this divine exchange. A flurry of interpretive inquiries arises from Jesus' logic: what interpretive assumptions and methods can support Jesus' approach to Ps 110? Are there similar moves made by other New Testament authors? Is there a model of Old Testament interpretation that can be drawn from this example?

The interpretive tool of "prosopological exegesis" has been a recent retrieval project determined to address these questions.[1] A robust definition will be provided below, but, in brief, prosopological exegesis is a "person-centered" interpretive approach, attempting to discern an unidentified character within a textual dialogue in order to illuminate the true speaker or addressee.[2] Though others have made excellent contributions, Matthew Bates is a leading scholar, trying to revive prosopological exegesis.[3] Following patristic authors such as Justin Martyr (c.100 –165), Irenaeus

---

[1] Works of theological retrieval are "what Rowan Williams calls 'creative archaeology,' attempts to dig into a past era in order to open up new vistas for today. Theologies of retrieval unsettle present discussions by offering resources from beyond the current horizon with a view toward enriching ongoing debates" (Darren Sarisky, "Introduction," in *Theologies of Retrieval: An Exploration and Appraisal*, ed. Darren Sarisky (London: T&T Clark, 2017), 2.

[2] Matthew W. Bates, *The Birth of the Trinity: Jesus, God, and the Spirit in New Testament and Early Christian Interpretations of the Old Testament* (Oxford: Oxford University Press, 2015), 34.

[3] Bates, *The Birth of the Trinity*. Also see Matthew W. Bates, *The Hermeneutics of Apostolic Proclamation: The Center of Paul's Method of Scriptural Interpretation* (Waco, TX: Baylor University Press, 2012); Madison Pierce, *Divine Discourse in the Epistle to the Hebrews: The Recontextualization of Spoken Quotations of Scripture* (Cambridge: Cambridge University Press, 2022); Kyle R. Hughes, *The Trinitarian Testimony of the Spirit*

(c.130–200), and Tertullian (c.160–c.220), who explicitly employed such a method, Bates winds back into the interpretive moves of New Testament authors and attempts to demonstrate biblical examples of prosopological exegesis (thus, PE). The supposed benefits of "person-centered" readings include satisfying interpretations of certain Old Testament dialogues, submission to New Testament hermeneutics, crucial conclusions for trinitarian theology, and evidence of a classical Christology. Though Bates' project and its offshoots have been generally well-received, there have been critiques from those who argue for a stronger typological interpretative approach.[4]

In light of the budding field of research surrounding PE and its criticism from some proponents of a robust typological and canonical method of exegesis, more work is needed in evaluating the history of interpretation concerning prosopological readings beyond the patristic period in order to understand if this "explanatory method" survived beyond the Middle Ages.[5] Some of the current critiques of PE resonate most comfortably with Reformation and Post-Reformation commitments to *sola scriptura* and broadly Reformed typological interpretation. Therefore, studies of exegetes within the Reformation and Post-Reformation traditions that evaluate the use or rejection of prosopological readings would provide fresh data for discerning the compatibility of PE within traditions that emphasize a typological hermeneutic across the canon.

To my knowledge, there are no studies available that focus on prosopological exegesis amongst Reformation and Post-Reformation theologians. This article then aims to utilize the eighteenth century Particular Baptist theologian John Gill (1697–1771) as a test case for the use of PE in the Post-Reformation tradition.[6] By exploring Gill's use of PE within his overarching Christocentric and typological approach to scripture, a dialogue partner is formed that demonstrates this explanatory method as a valuable part of the Post-Reformation interpretive tradition, particularly in its construction of Christology, and offers challenges and continuity to both Bates and his critics. Furthermore, Gill sees typology as the first layer of contact between an Old Testament text and its New Testament antitype, but when the textual dialogue and/or its New Testament interpretation demands a stronger correlation, Gill does not hesitate to argue for a prosopological solution. These conclusions will be argued in five moves: by introducing the current retrieval project of PE and its conflicts with typological interpretation; presenting the relevant critiques of prosopological interpretation from various proponents of a typology-centered approach; offering Gill as a prime model for

---

(Leiden, the Netherlands: Brill, 2018).

4 David Schrock, "Reading the Psalms with the Church: A Critical Evaluation of Prosopological Exegesis in Light of Church History," *The Southern Baptist Journal of Theology* 10.3 (2021): 77–96; Peter J. Gentry, "A Preliminary Evaluation and Critique of Prosopological Exegesis," *The Southern Baptist Journal of Theology* 23.2 (2019): 105–22; William James Dernell, "Typology, Christology, and Prosopological Exegesis: Implicit Narratives in Christological Texts," *The Southern Baptist Journal of Theology* 24.1 (2020): 137–61; Dernell, "Typology, Christology and Prosopological Exegesis: Implicit Narratives in Christological Texts," *The Southern Baptist Journal of Theology* 24.1 (2020): 137–61; James M. Hamilton, Jr., *Typology: Understanding the Bible's Promise-Shaped Patterns* (Grand Rapids: Zondervan, 2022), 144–6.

5 Bates, *Birth of the Trinity*, 3.

6 More defence of Gill as a suitable example of Reformed theology and interpretation will be provided below, but, in short, Willem Van Asselt describes Gill as "one of the most important representatives of Reformed scholasticism in the eighteenth century" (Van Asselt, *Introduction to Reformed Scholasticism* [Grand Rapids, MI: Reformation Heritage Books, 2011], 179).

analyzing PE within the Reformed tradition; examining Gill's interpretation of specific texts that are possible examples of PE and their contributions to Christology; and providing a few concluding reflections from Gill's data that interact with the current discussion on Bates' influential retrieval project of a person-centered approach for biblical interpretation.

Prosopological Exegesis in Recent Discussion
Matthew Bates' Retrieval of PE
The genesis of Bates' reintroduction of this explanatory method is found in his *The Hermeneutics of the Apostolic Proclamation* (2012), in which his aim was to demonstrate that "Paul received, utilized, and extended an apostolic, kerygmatic narrative tradition centered on certain key events in the Christ story as his primary interpretative lens—a narrative tradition that already contained a built-in hermeneutic."[7] Such a "Christocentric narrative tradition" submitted to by Paul "articulated a fundamental hermeneutical posture."[8] In exploring how such an overarching hermeneutic was applied, Bates argues that prosopological interpretation was one of Paul's tools for demonstrating this Christocentric narrative tradition in the Scriptures. Bates defines PE as "a reading technique whereby an interpreter seeks to overcome a real or perceived ambiguity regarding the identity of the speakers or addressees (or both) in the divinely inspired source text by assigning nontrivial *prosopa* (i.e., nontrivial vis-à-vis the 'plain sense' of the text) to the speakers or addressees (or both) in order to make sense of the text."[9] Bates summarizes his criteria for discerning the need for a prosopological reading as follows: (i) speech or dialogue, (ii) non-triviality of person (i.e., ambiguous), (iii) priority of introductory formulae or markers, and (iiii) intertextual evidence.[10] Alongside the use of PE in patristic sources, Bates analyzes potential uses of prosopological interpretation in Paul's corpus and concludes that such a "technique is disproportionately vital to understanding Paul's Christology, hermeneutic, and conception of the Father-Son-Spirit relationship."[11]

In his *The Birth of the Trinity* (2015), Bates broadens his claim of Pauline reliance on PE in promoting a high Christology and Father-Son-Spirit relations to a New Testament wide utilization of PE that resulted in the formulation of divine person language in the early church, or as he provocatively puts it, "prosopological exegesis…was irreducibly essential to the birth of the Trinity."[12] He argues that early Christians engaged in an "explanatory method" also present in Jewish and Greco-Roman sources that assigned

---

7 Bates, *Hermeneutics of Apostolic Proclamation*, 56.

8 Bates, *Hermeneutics of Apostolic Proclamation*, 57.

9 Bates, *Hermeneutics of Apostolic Proclamation*, 217.

10 Bates, *Hermeneutics of Apostolic Proclamation*, 221.

11 Bates, *Hermeneutics of Apostolic Proclamation*, 326.

12 Bates, *Birth of the Trinity*, 2. He tones down the rhetoric of his title two pages later: "As such, in speaking of 'the birth of the Trinity,' I do not refer to the ultimate 'real' or ontological starting point for the Trinity traditionally, Christians have affirmed that the triune God is eternal, with no origin in time, and this study ultimately finds much early Christian testimony to support that claim. Rather, in speaking of" the birth of the Trinity, I refer to the arrival and initial sociolinguistic framing of this doctrine in human history by the nascent church" (Bates, *Birth of the Trinity* 4).

characters to "ambivalent speeches in inspired texts."[13] By recognizing that Old Testament prophets were engaged in presenting a "grand theodrama" by occasionally "taking on various *prosopa* (persons, masks, characters)," New Testament authors and early Christians could more clearly identify these characters in light of fuller revelation in their privileged time within redemptive history.[14] When this prosopological reading strategy is illuminated amongst the New Testament authors, a robust theology of divine persons is unveiled in the Old Testament and a high Christology is made evident that counters claims of unnatural dogmatic formulations of trinitarianism and Christology by later tradition.[15]

Working off his previous formulation of a prosopological method, Bates identifies three settings within the "theo-drama" or divine economy, which are the prophetic setting, the theo-dramatic setting, and the actualized setting.[16] The prophetic setting is the "horizon of the time and the circumstances of the prophet in ancient Israel."[17] The theo-dramatic setting is the time at which the speech is set in the larger "divine play" or "theo-drama."[18] For example, if David takes on the character of Christ in a speech that is clearly located from the cross, then the theo-dramatic setting would be the event of the crucifixion.[19] The actualized setting is the time when the theo-drama is "truly performed" by the character the prophet was personifying in the theo-drama.[20]

Though early Christian readers may not have been self-conscious of the methods and nomenclature of PE, they are engaged in the practice by "dialogically" reading Israel's one God as "differentiated persons" in the Old Testament.[21] Bates contends that prosopological exegetes in the early church and New Testament upheld the authorial intent of the Old Testament prophets by believing the prophets "willingly participated in a theodramatic speech-performance, yet they simply may not have fully understood the significance of the role-playing or the full meaning of the prophetic utterance in light of the entire divine economy."[22] The upshot of these "solution-by-person" readings is the illumination of divine conversations that "are like shafts of heavenly light shooting

---

13 Bates, *Birth of the Trinity*, 3.

14 Bates, *Birth of the Trinity*, 5.

15 Bates, *Birth of the Trinity*, 7.

16 Bates, *Birth of the Trinity*, 34–35.

17 Bates, *Birth of the Trinity*, 34.

18 Bates, *Birth of the Trinity*, 34.

19 Bates, *Birth of the Trinity*, 34.

20 Bates, *Birth of the Trinity*, 35. Bates makes an important point on the actualized setting that "Note that because the theodramatic setting is chronologically unrestrained (past, present, or future) with respect to the prophetic setting, the actualized setting is likewise unrestrained. In this way the whole chronological spectrum of the divine economy may be involved in any given prophetic utterance" (Bates, *Birth of the Trinity*, 35).

21 Bates, *Birth of the Trinity*, 63, 85. For second century interpreters, Pierce argues prosopological exegesis could have been much more methodologically self-conscious: "While this formal training (and its terminology) might be confined to the elite in society, it is likely that these principles would dissipate to the wider public, which is why Justin can assume that his readers would be able to use prosopological exegesis also" (Pierece, *Divine Discourse in the Epistle to the Hebrews*, 8).

22 Bates, *Birth of the Trinity*, 192.

through the cloudy sky of our earthly sojourn" that provide footage of the Trinity's life *ad intra* and the triune God's missions *ad extra*.[23] Bates makes his claim that PE of the Old Testament found in the New Testament and early church are theologically load-bearing by arguing that it is this procedure that gave the early church organic language for speaking of one God in three persons and produced the terminology of *person* language that would later flower in Nicene orthodoxy and creedal Christology.[24] He goes so far as to say regardless of how one judges the legitimacy of this method, the early church's "theology is ultimately inseparable from the technique."[25] In other words, the early church and the New Testament's PE "offered a triune key to these interpretative locks."[26]

Tensions with Typology
In various places, Bates interacts with the use of typology in intertextual analysis.[27] He makes clear his disagreement with the broad consensus of typology as the supposed interpretive practice of the early church in texts where divine discourse is attributed to Old Testament passages by New Testament authors and argues for PE as the real strategy of New Testament interpretation in these instances.[28] One of his direct interactions is with Richard Hays and Bates makes crucial nuances for his critique of typology:

> Although there is plenty of reasoning around "types" in the New Testament in general (and Hays is an outstanding guide), the typological model as applied to the special case of Christ as one who speaks in the Old Testament, in my judgment, has decisive weaknesses--especially the lack of evidence that the earliest Christians had sufficient interest in the suffering of David so as to provide an imitative link. Accordingly, this book, by way of the cumulative force of the examples presented and evidence from reception history, seeks to advocate for a new way of understanding the interpretative logic of the earliest church: When the Christ was found to speak or to be addressed in the Old Testament, this was generally because the first Christians were reading these particular texts in a prosopological rather than typological fashion.[29]

First, Bates is not dismissing typology as an unwarranted pattern or practice in scripture. Second, his critique limits its scope to texts where PE is an interpretive

---

23 Bates, *Birth of the Trinity*, 41, 136.

24 Bates, *Birth of the Trinity*, 175.

25 Bates, *Birth of the Trinity*, 83–84.

26 Bates, *Birth of the Trinity*, 84.

27 Bates summarizes the concept of typology he engages with in the example of David as presented by Richard Hays: "Richard Hays, believes that David was regarded by the early church as a type or pattern for the future Christ, while at the same time, because the king embodied Israel's national sorrows and hopes he was also a type in the sense of a corporate symbol, allowing early Christians to see an imitative correspondence between David, Israel, and the future Christ" (Bates, *Birth of the Trinity*, 9).

28 Bates, *Birth of the Trinity*, 9.

29 Bates, *Birth of the Trinity*, 9.

option, meaning it meets the criteria outlined above. Third, Bates' critique involves the argument that New Testament and early church interpreters of the Psalms were not concerned with typologically arguing for similarities between the lives of David and Christ. Fourth, the apparent dissimilarity of David and Christ favors PE over typological correspondence. For example, Bates contends that Paul's use of Ps 16:10 stating that Acts 13:34 testifies to the fulfilled promise of Christ's resurrection discourages readers from typologically linking David and Christ in this speech because Paul rules out David as having been the recipient of its fulfilment (Acts 13:36).[30] Yet Christ truly sees its accomplishment in his life (Acts 13:37).

The larger critique of typological readings is wrapped up in Bates' frustration with typology as a discipline within Pauline studies and his acceptable criteria for a biblical "type."[31] He is emphatic that "throughout the Pauline corpus there is no interest in the pattern of suffering/vindication in the life of David that would seem to be necessary" to warrant typological readings.[32] The imitation necessary for typology is one of "iconic mimesis," the explanation of typology Bates adheres to.[33] The disqualification of typology in the Davidic Psalms where Bates finds PE to be present is demonstrated by the fact that "a type demands that the respective Old Testament and New Testament passages participate in a common image (iconic mimesis), and the prosopological reasoning is precisely that the actors do not appropriately share that image."[34] In short, "David himself cannot supply the image because the words do not correspond to David's own experiences" in examples such as Acts 13.[35] In light of this elimination of typological interpretation in these passages, Bates offers a simple formula––"if not the ancient prophet, then a theodramatic character."[36] When the prophet's life does not match the speech, then a divine person can be tried as a better fit. For textual evidence, Bates insists this exact logic is at play by Peter and Paul in Acts 2:29–36 and Acts 13:36–37, and this formula employed by the apostles discourages a typological correspondence in these prophetic Psalms between David and Christ.[37]

Critiques of Bates' Qualms with Typology
As noted above, the criticisms of Bates I intend to interact with are by those who are committed to typological interpretation and appreciate the Reformation and Post-Reformation exegetical tradition. First, Jim Hamilton sporadically makes dialogues with Bates' approach throughout his *Typology* (2022). In "Prosopology or Typology?," Hamilton contrasts his idea with Bates' over the application, in Heb 2:12, of Jesus

30 Bates, *Birth of the Trinity*, 71–72.

31 Bates, *Hermeneutics of Apostolic Proclamation*, 251n72.

32 Bates, *Hermeneutics of Apostolic Proclamation*, 250.

33 Bates, *Birth of the Trinity*, 72. See Frances M. Young, *Biblical Exegesis and the Formation of Christian Culture* (Peabody, MA: Hendrickson, 2002), 192–201; Bates, *Hermeneutics of the Apostolic Proclamation*, 133–8.

34 Bates, *Birth of the Trinity*, 182–3.

35 Bates, *Birth of the Trinity*, 72.

36 Bates, *Birth of the Trinity*, 182.

37 Bates, *Birth of the Trinity*, 182.

"saying" the words of Ps 22 and Isa 8:17–18.[38] For Hamilton, Bates' prosopological reading "vitiates the meaning of the text in its Old Testament context" by making the author of Hebrews engage in "an arbitrary, non-contextual, exegetically unwarranted interpretive practice whereby he simply makes the text of the Old Testament say what he wants it to say."[39] Even though the author of Hebrews applies the words to Christ, Hamilton warns that the author "does not spell out the rationale for that presentation."[40] The audience of Hebrews would be aware of the original context of Ps 22 and Isaiah leading them to reject a prosopological insertion, and this would betray the typological argument the author makes throughout its apologetic for Christ.[41] Figures like David and Isaiah are ripe with typological connection to Jesus as they represent the collective seed of the woman (Gen 3:15).[42] The rub for Hamilton is Bates' supposed refusal to respect the original context of Old Testament texts and assertion of the New Testament authors' similar lack of exegetical interest.[43] For Hamilton, Bates only concerns how the early church interpreted a given text while, whereas he prioritizes how the author and final form intended its meaning.[44] From this framing of their differences, Hamilton concludes that faithful interpretation will unveil typological connection between David and Christ in passages such as Ps 22, not prosopological readings.[45]

A second critique is by David Schrock, who takes a more systematic and historical approach than Hamilton does. One of Schrock's main complaints is that Bates' retrieval of PE under the banner of pre-critical hermeneutics is a combination of "modern commitments with ancient practices, all the while advocating a postmodern commitment to the interpretive community."[46] His positive claim is that typological interpretation of the Psalms is more adequate for producing a classical Christology than PE.[47] In defence of his critique, Schrock argues that "PE rejects a typological reading of

---

38 Hamilton, *Typology*, 144.

39 Hamilton, *Typology*, 144.

40 Hamilton, *Typology*, 144.

41 Hamilton, *Typology*, 144–5.

42 Hamilton, *Typology*, 145.

43 Hamilton, *Typology*, 175–6.

44 Hamilton, *Typology*, 181.

45 Hamilton, *Typology*, 181, 197. A similar critique is made by Peter Gentry, who believes PE is anachronistic. For Gentry, PE does not "account for apostolic reasoning from the Bible's storyline, the horizons of interpretation, and the predictive and prophetic nature of typology. The main problem is that if the NT authors are claiming things that an OT text does not clearly intend in its contexts (original, epochal, canonical), then the issue of warrant disappears, and you are never able to show from the OT itself that it was leading us to the NT conclusion. *Sensus literalis* is tied to divine and human authorial intent in the text, and it is especially important to think through how later authors of the OT are building on earlier authors, which is all authorial intent. One must show that the NT authors are getting the authorial intent correctly. And if they are not getting that intent correctly, then they are reading in things that they have no basis to show from the OT. If this is so, how would they prove to a Jewish person that Jesus is the fulfillment of the OT? They are arguing from the Scriptures. They are not making things up" (Gentry, "A Preliminary Evaluation and Critique of Prosopological Exegesis," 120).

46 Schrock, "Reading the Psalms with the Church," 78.

47 Schrock, "Reading the Psalms with the Church," 78–79.

Scripture as a modern invention of the Enlightenment."[48] In evaluating Bates, Schrock admits he relies on Craig Carter's summary and sees Carter in harmony: "In the end, typology is a modern solution to a modern problem and we would be wise to heed Bates warning not to 'foist our peculiar modern notions of history and referentiality onto Paul.' Modern concepts of typology serve more to mask the problem then to solve it."[49] Based on this modern, anti-supernatural understanding of typology, Schrock claims Bates insists on PE as a better option.[50] If Bates is rejecting typology based on historical-critical flavors of it and without considering conceptions of typology from those who have an inspired and canonical approach to the scriptures, then Bates is throwing the "baby out with the bathwater."[51]

Schrock's another criticism is that Bates "builds his entire approach to Scripture on the fact that later texts and interpreters (i.e., reception history) can and should inform the meaning of earlier texts" and allowing tradition to inform exegesis.[52] For Schrock,

> [PE] threatens the canonical enterprise of interpreting Scripture with Scripture. The Reformation principle of Sola Scriptura leads us to read the text on its own terms and not to define the terms of Scripture by the later traditions of the church. This dependence on later traditions (i.e., reception history) is what the Reformation stood against, and it is something that stands against PE too. We will consider this further below, but for now, it is important to recognize how seismic Bates' proposal is. What is at stake is not just the interpretation of a few verses, although interpretation of the Psalms is at issue. What is at stake are the principles of the Reformation itself.[53]

Thus, according to Schrock, PE attacks *sola scriptura* on two fronts. It is seen as an incognito higher critical method that attempts to find a voice or a "pre-history" behind the text even if it is a divine person in eternity.[54] It also subverts the practice of scripture interpreting scripture by requiring "creedal statements to provide the orthodox interpretation of passages like Psalm 2 and Psalm 110."[55] In the final analysis, Schrock argues, in a similar vein to Hamilton, that the original context takes priority, and this context will result in a typological reading that corresponds to its New Testament citations contrary to the claims of PE. The difference for Schrock is his framing of the issue as a battle for fidelity to *sola scriptura*.[56]

---

48 Schrock, "Reading the Psalms with the Church," 86.

49 Schrock, "Reading the Psalms with the Church," 86. See Craig A. Carter, *Interpreting Scripture with the Great Tradition: Recovering the Genius of Premodern Exegesis* (Grand Rapids, MI: Baker, 2018), 196.

50 Schrock, "Reading the Psalms with the Church," 86.

51 Schrock, "Reading the Psalms with the Church," 89.

52 Schrock, "Reading the Psalms with the Church," 88–89.

53 Schrock, "Reading the Psalms with the Church," 89.

54 Schrock, "Reading the Psalms with the Church," 89–90.

55 Schrock, "Reading the Psalms with the Church," 90.

56 Schrock, "Reading the Psalms with the Church," 91.

These critiques have their strengths. Hamilton's insistence on mining the original context for all its worth before turning to later interpretations is responsible exegesis. Schrock's complaint that Bates never considers proponents of typological interpretation that are also committed to inspiration and canonical unity is warranted. Yet there are problems with each author's criticism that point out the need for searching the Reformation and Post-Reformation tradition for more dialogue on PE. Both authors admit passages like Heb 2 and Heb 10 explicitly place the words of Davidic Psalms in the mouth of Christ yet provide no direct answers that deal with the force of these assertions by the author of Hebrews directly; instead, typological connections are provided between David and Christ, but not solutions to Christ actually speaking them. Second, Schrock's argument that Bates rejects typology outright as a modern phenomenon is simply false. As outlined above, Bates considers typology and concedes that it is a scriptural practice even if he is hesitant of its dominance in biblical studies.[57] Third, the claim by both critics that Bates has the New Testament authors engage in arbitrary interpretation of prophetic texts ignores his nuance of the prophetic, theo-dramatic, and actualized settings along with the ambiguities of the speakers in some of these Old Testament passages that are presented as in need of clarification. Lastly, Schrock's claim that PE violates the Reformation principle of *Sola Scriptura* can be challenged by the presence of PE in the works of Reformation and Post-Reformation theologians themselves.[58] Bates' project and these critiques set up nicely the addition of another dialogue partner who sheds light on these conflicts, a user of PE who embodies pre-critical hermeneutics, classical trinitarianism, a high Christology, typological interpretation, and stands among the great theologians of the Post-Reformation period, John Gill.

John Gill as PE Test Case

Before detailing his examples of PE, it is necessary to explain why John Gill is a relevant subject for this discussion and what his overall hermeneutics are. First, Gill, an eighteenth-century London Particular Baptist pastor and theologian, was a pre-critical interpreter, who employed Christocentricism in his hermeneutics.[59] Gill's "classical Christian exegesis" coupled with a high Christology adjudicate "questions of larger theological reference."[60] Second, Gill was a serious exegete and systematician. Among his works were nine volumes of exegetical commentary on the entire Bible

---

57 Even Carter, whom Schrock relies on, notes that "Bates ... does see Paul as using typology language to refer to 'deliberately anticipatory types' in the Old Testament" (Carter, *Interpreting Scripture*, 167).

58 In addition, the accusation that Bates reads tradition back into these texts to find classical trinitarianism and creedal Christology is unwarranted. Bates' appeals to evidence of divine persons in the Psalms and Prophets are predominantly driven by their New Testament interpretations, i.e., scripture interpreting scripture.

59 Raymond C. Ortlund, "John Gill as Interpreter of the Old Testament," in *The Life and Thought of John Gill (1697–1771): A Tercentennial Appreciation*, ed. Michael A.G. Haykin (Leiden, the Netherlands: Brill, 1997), 97, 110.

60 Ortlund, "John Gill as Interpreter," 97. Orltund states that Gill was "fortunate to live in a time before the Christological theology of the text was squinted at as inadmissible in accredited exegetical procedure," and he "saw the Old Testament as authentic in its present form, faithfully representing its own origins and unified in its message" (Ortlund, "John Gill as Interpreter," 109–10).

and his body of divinity, which was penned after his commentaries.[61] Third, Gill was a Reformed theologian. It may seem strange to speak this way about a Baptist theologian of the eighteenth century, but it is fully justified after a scan of Gill's sources and his works.[62] Willem Van Asselt describes Gill as "one of the most important representatives of Reformed scholasticism in the eighteenth century."[63] Richard Muller records a handful of Gill's typical citations that overwhelmingly saturate him in the Reformed heritage.[64] In both "biblical interpretation" and "theological construction," Gill attempts to "maintain exegetical continuity" with the Reformed orthodox of the seventeenth century.[65] As Muller states:

> This brief survey of Gill's sources indicates that, after the Bible, the main positive points of reference for Gill's theology were the great Reformed and Puritan writers of the seventeenth century. The point is important for several reasons. In the first place, it locates Gill in relation to the Reformed dogmatic tradition, specifically, the tradition of Puritanism and its continental analogue, post-Reformation Reformed orthodoxy.[66]

The most fruitful instance of Gill's thought on method is found in his preface to the commentary on the Prophets, which was the first Old Testament commentary Gill produced.[67] After outlining the divine inspiration and diverse manners of delivery in the prophets, he calls readers to submit to Christ's teaching of his disciples to search for him in the scriptures as Christ is "the principal subject, scope, and centre of them."[68] In fact, "every evangelic truth" concerning Christ's person and work is witnessed to by the prophets.[69] Gill sees a narration of Christ's person and mission embedded in the Psalms and Prophets, as "it seems no very difficult task, by joining at least the book of Psalms with the Prophets, to extract out of them a narrative of the person, character, birth, life, actions, sufferings, and death of Christ; his burial, resurrection, ascension, and session

---

61 These commentaries were serious scholarship, as Gill had extensive notes utilizing biblical languages, the Targums, textual criticism archaeology, church fathers, continental reformers, Puritan divines, ancient philosophy, and more.

62 For broader affirmation of Particular Baptists' place within Reformed theology, see Matthew C. Bingham, *Orthodox Radicals: Baptist Identity in the English Revolution* (New York: Oxford University Press, 2019).

63 Van Asselt, *Introduction to Reformed Scholasticism*, 179.

64 Richard A. Muller, "John Gill and the Reformed Tradition: A Study in the Reception of Protestant Orthodoxy in the Eighteenth Century," in *Life and Thought of John Gill*, 53–54.

65 Richard A. Muller, *Post-Reformation Reformed Dogmatics: The Rise and Development of Reformed Orthodoxy*, rev. ed. (Grand Rapids, MI: Baker, 2003), 3:150.

66 Muller, "John Gill and the Reformed Tradition," 53–54.

67 John Gill, *An Exposition of the Old Testament* (London: Mathews and Leigh, 1810), 5:iii–xi.

68 Gill, *Exposition of the Old Testament*, 5:vi–vii.

69 Gill, *Exposition of the Old Testament*, 5:vii. The "evangelic truths" are what Gill defines as the rule of faith. For his own outline of this rule, see John Gill, "Sermon VIII: The Agreement of the Old and the New Testament," in *A Collection of Sermons and Tracts* (London, 1773), 1:122–37.

at the right hand of God, and second coming to judgment."[70]

With his overarching Christocentric commitments in place, Gill faces interpretive challenges in the Prophets through meditation, prayer, and "by comparing Scripture with Scripture, especially with the writings of the New Testament, and particularly the book of the Revelation; and there are some general rules, which, if attended to, will greatly facilitate the understanding of them."[71] The rules Gill has in mind are those outlined by Campegius Vitringa (1659–1722), a Dutch Reformed scholastic, who produced substantial commentaries on Isaiah and other prophetic books.[72] Gill admits deep admiration of Vitringa for rules of interpretation in regards to Old Testament prophecy.[73] The following session will only mention the tenants relevant to the discussion of PE and typology.

Rule one and two insist that the subject of the prophecy must first be determined, the time of the events must be discerned, and if the prophet speaks of this subject "properly and literally, or improperly and figuratively."[74] The second rule states that the subject of the prophecy can be discerned by the attributes spoken of him if the subject is not named, or, if the subject is named, it should be discerned "whether it is to be taken properly or mystically; or partly properly, and partly mystically; as when any one by name is spoken of as a type of the Messiah."[75] For Gill, even a named subject can be spoken mystically of another, namely, of the Messiah of which they are possibly a type. As long as the subject of the "literal" sense is named and it agrees with the characteristics ascribed to it, interpreters should not look for another character, but a subject whose characteristics do not fit should prompt a search for another actor.[76] The explicitly named subject of a prophecy may contain both a "proper and mystical

---

70 Gill, *Exposition of the Old Testament*, 5:vii–viii. Ortlund remarks that "as a Christian interpreter, Gill saw the Old Testament in organic unity with the New, leading up to the appearing of Jesus Christ, the fulfillment of the whole. To Gill, the worldview of the Bible could be thought of as spherical, filled with one body of truth. Christ is the great central theme integrating the whole; and yet each particular passage in Scripture, from Genesis to Revelation, offers itself to the reader as a window on the surface of that sphere, each aperture disclosing to the discerning reader a unique angle of vision into the central christological theme. This hermeneutical sense of the theological substructure underlying the text enables Gill's exegesis to be both stable and (usually) interesting, for it persuades him that the Scriptures are indeed unified and also allows him to venture forth into passage-specific exegesis rather than timidly hang back in an unimaginative Systematics. In this respect, Gill's work is of a piece with the mainstream of the best Reformation and Puritan interpreters" (Ortlund, "John Gill as Interpreter," 110–1).

71 Gill, *Exposition of the Old Testament*, 5:viii.

72 Campegius Vitringa, *Aanleiding tot het recht Verstant van den Tempel, die de prophet Ezechiel bezien en beschreeven heft* (Franeker, 1687); idem, *Commentarius in librum prophetiarum Jesaiae* (Herborn, 1722); idem, *Anacrisis Apocalypseos Joannis Apostoli qua in veras interpretandae ejus hypotheses diligenter inquiritur et ex iisdern interpretatio facta, certis historiarurn rnonurnentis confirrnarnur atque illustratur; ea etiarn quae Meldensis praesul Bossuetus in hujus vaticinii cornrnentario supposuit, et exegetico protestantiurn systernati in visis de bestia ac baby/one rnystica objecit, sedulo exarninantur* (Franeker, 1705). The influence of these commentaries reaches into the eighteenth and early nineteenth centuries. See Brevard S. Childs, "Hermeneutical Reflections on Campegius Vitringa, Eighteenth-Century Interpreter of Isaiah," in *In Search of True Wisdom: Essays in Old Testament Interpretation in Honour of Ronald E. Clements*, ed. Edward Ball (Sheffield: Sheffield Academic, 1999), 90; Charles Telfer, *Wrestling with Isaiah: The Exegetical Methodology of Campegius Vitringa (1659–1722)* (Göttingen: Vandenhoeck & Ruprecht, 2016).

73 Gill, *Exposition of the Old Testament*, 5:viii, x.

74 Gill, *Exposition of the Old Testament*, 5:viii.

75 Gill, *Exposition of the Old Testament*, 5:viii.

76 Gill, *Exposition of the Old Testament*, 5:viii.

interpretation" where some aspects agree with the mystical interpretation "and others are more rightly predicated of it, in a literal and grammatic sense" as the mystical sense is "wrapped up in the literal sense."[77] The subject must be understood as "complex," which the prophet, guided by the Spirit, would have comprehended.[78]

Gill's description of rule eleven is telling. He argues for a true knowledge of Christ as the "key" to interpreting prophecy.[79] Those that rarely find Christ in the prophetic texts are "barren" while those that frequently find Christ are fruitful because the Spirit of Christ is in the prophets and speaks of himself; therefore, "it is the business of a good interpreter, first indeed to seek diligently after Christ in the prophetic word; then, if occasion favours, to demonstrate it; but never to shun any opportunity, when it offers itself, but willingly take it."[80] The use of the key of Christ is demonstrated for interpreters by the interpretations of Christ himself and the rest of the New Testament authors. Their readings of Old Testament texts lead us "to the true understanding of those oracles."[81] Emphasis on the spiritual sense can be had without doing violence to the Old Testament text. Gill offers his linguistic work, historical and geographical knowledge, and use of scripture interpreting scripture as evidence of his commitment to exegeting the text in its original context.[82] Gill's Christocentric interpretive key, emphasis on typology, and insistence on determining subjects of prophesy according to their agreement with the characteristics assigned to them set up nicely our investigation of PE in his corpus in light of the current discussion in theological and biblical studies. His interpretations of the Psalms will be surveyed for his application of these principles along with his use of PE.

Gill's PE of the Psalms

In his preface to his commentary on the Psalms, Gill declares that many psalms speak of the person, offices, and work of Christ along with a "rich mine of … evangelical truths."[83] A perusal of this work will quickly expose a heavy diet of typology where Gill is constantly correlating types (person, places, institutions, or events) to a supposed antitype, either Christ or the church. Yet in the midst of this typological approach, there are times when Gill applies another solution to the task of determining a prophetic subject, PE. Of course, a detailed method akin to modern discussions of criteria concerning PE will not be found in Gill, but the evident practice and the logic behind it can be. For Gill, the most succinct description of this phenomenon in prophetic texts is what he calls "personating." Confirmed by the attribution of the words of Ps 40 to Christ in Heb 10:5–10, David is "personating the Messiah."[84] Asaph "personated Christ" in Ps

---

77 Gill, *Exposition of the Old Testament*, 5:viii–ix.

78 Gill, *Exposition of the Old Testament*, 5:viii–ix.

79 Gill, *Exposition of the Old Testament*, 5:ix.

80 Gill, *Exposition of the Old Testament*, 5:ix.

81 Gill, *Exposition of the Old Testament*, 5:ix–x.

82 Gill, *Exposition of the Old Testament*, 5:x.

83 John Gill, *An Exposition of the Old Testament* (London: Mathews and Leigh, 1810), 3:524.

84 John Gill, *A Complete Body of Doctrinal and Practical Divinity: Or A System of Evangelical Truths,*

78 in light of the placement of the psalm in Christ's mouth in Matt 13:34–35.[85] Even as a correlated "type of Christ," David "seems, throughout the whole, to personate him" in Ps 101.[86] Gill sees evidence of a prosopological reading in Paul's use of Ps 18:49 in Rom 15, where these "words are not spoken unto God by David, literally considered, but as personating the Messiah."[87] Gill's explanation of Isa 49 summarizes the mechanics of the prophet's function in these texts; the prophecy is "delivered out by the prophet, in the person of Christ."[88] Other examples of Psalms where Gill sees the person of Christ speaking directly through the prophet's "personation" include Pss 16, 17, 69, 109.

Is there any rhyme or rhythm as to when Gill claims a prophet is "personating?" A few observations may provide clarity. An important interpretive foundation for Gill's Christocentric reading of the Psalms is how he attributes entire Psalms to Christ. Gill's conviction that Christ is the sole speaker in most of Psalm 16 based on what he believes is a prosopological reading of this text by the apostles in Acts 2:25–31 and 13:35–37 leads him to conclude the "whole of the psalm must be interpreted of him."[89] Gill invokes the same principle in light of the prophetic speech in Ps 41 concerning Christ and the betrayal of Judas Iscariot cited by John 13:18: "having such a sure rule of interpretation, we may safely venture to explain the whole psalm of Christ, which treats both of his humiliation and exaltation; for it neither agrees with David wholly, nor with Hezekiah, to whom some ascribe it."[90] In other words, discerning a New Testament designation of the psalmist's words to Christ and a discontinuity with characteristics of the original speaker are a key principle for identifying Christocentric Psalms. Conversely, a Psalm that is Christocentric provides confidence for a possible prosopological interpretation of its parts.

As for the supposed antithesis between typology and PE, Gill mostly exemplifies the opposite. In one of the most discussed passages on PE--Ps 22--Gill interprets it prosopologically and even makes references to early Christians authors such as Justin Martyr and Tertullian, while still calling David a "type of Christ."[91] For Gill, typology and prosopology can exist in the same text. Evidence of typology does not rule out PE in Gill's mind. On Ps 17, Gill considers the prayer to be either in "his [David] own person ... or in the person of the Messiah," but either way David is still a type in Ps 17, since his circumstances of being persecuted by Saul match Christ's sufferings.[92] Yet there are certain textual situations when Gill keeps distance from prosopological interpretation, as he sees typology not meeting the exegetical needs of certain Psalms

---

Deduced from the Sacred Scriptures, rev. ed. (London, 1839), 1:324–5.

85 Gill, *Exposition of the Old Testament*, 4:24–25.

86 Gill, *Exposition of the Old Testament*, 4: 123.

87 John Gill, *An Exposition of the New Testament* (London: Mathews and Leigh, 1809), 2:572–3. Gill believes David can also personate the church. See Gill, *Exposition of the Old Testament*, 3:779–82, 822.

88 Gill, *Exposition of the Old Testament*, 5:283

89 Gill, *Exposition of the Old Testament*, 3:581.

90 Gill, *Exposition of the Old Testament*, 3:698.

91 Gill, *Exposition of the Old Testament*, 3:616.

92 Gill, *Exposition of the Old Testament*, 3:586.

that speak in unique ways about Christ's divinity, sonship, and ultimate mission.

Psalm 2

Psalm 2 is the subject of great debate in formulations of Christology, particularly regarding the deity and eternal generation of the Son. The theological consequences of interpreting Ps 2:7 were not peripheral issues for Gill.[93] Therefore, he took great care in exegeting this passage along with its use in Christology. He opens his discussion of Ps 2 in his commentary by contending that it describes the Messiah, since many parts of the psalm agree with the characteristics of Christ over the life of David.[94] The mediatorial God-man in the passion narrative in Ps 2:1–6 applies to Christ's suffering and glorification.[95] With Heb 1, Gill understands that the direct speech of the Son recounting the words of his Father is the circumstance of Ps 2:7.[96] Christ reminds the Father of his decree that "you are my Son; today I have begotten you." The date of "today" is set in eternity as an "everlasting now" and is manifested at "any time and case in which Christ is declared to be the Son of God."[97] In Ps 2:8–9, the Father responds to the Son by recounting his offer of all things to the Son and declares the Son will rule and conquer. For Gill, it is a transcript of the eternal council of the triune God in the redemptive covenant, and he ascribes the reward of ruling with "a rod of iron" to the depiction of Christ in Rev 2:27, 12:5, and 19:15.[98]

Gill draws a couple of conclusions from this person-centered reading:

> He [Christ] was a Son previous to his being Prophet, Priest, and King; and his office is not the foundation of his sonship, but his sonship is the foundation of his office; or by which that is supported, and which fits him for the performance of it: but it has respect to his person; for, as in human generation, person begets person, and like begets like, so in divine generation; but care must be taken to remove all imperfection from it, such as divisibility and multiplication of essence, priority and posteriority, dependence, and the like: nor can the modus or manner of it be conceived or explained by us.[99]

First, since Christ's eternal sonship is prior to his mediatorial office and mission, to argue for adoptionism, based on Christ's resurrection, is invalid.[100] Second, the

---

93 For a thorough account of Gill's engagement in the theology of divine sonship, see Jonathan Elliot Swan, "The Fountain of Life": John Gill's Doctrine of Christ's Eternal Sonship" (PhD diss., The Southern Baptist Theological Seminary, 2021); idem, "John Gill (1697–1771) and the Eternal Begotten Word of God," in *In Essence One, In Persons Three: The Doctrine of the Trinity in Particular Baptist Life and Thought 1640s–1840s*, ed. Michael A.G. Haykin and Roy M. Paul (West Lorne, ON: H&E, 2022), 69–98.

94 Gill, *Exposition of the Old Testament*, 3:528.

95 Gill, *Exposition of the Old Testament*, 3:528–30.

96 Gill, *Exposition of the Old Testament*, 3:530. Bates calls the exchange in Ps 2:7 a "theodrama within a theodrama" (Bates, *Birth of the Trinity*, 67–68).

97 Gill, *Exposition of the Old Testament*, 3:531.

98 Gill, *Exposition of the Old Testament*, 3:531.

99 Gill, *Exposition of the Old Testament*, 3:531.

100 Swan, "The Fountain of Life," 137. The insistence of the early church on eternal divine discourse between the Father and Son drawn out by Bates for defending against adoptionism is exactly what Gill is

begetting of the Son is a generation of person, not divisible essence. Therefore, there is one divine essence, but multiple divine persons distinguished by relations of origin. The clarity of unpacking such a divine conversation between the Father and Son along with its christological consequences relies upon Gill's distancing of David from the possibility of being the typological character in Ps 2. Gill makes a more explicit move in his comments on Ps 18:49 and its use in Rom 15. When David states "for this I will praise you, O Lord, among the nations, and sing to your name," he is "personating the Messiah," as David is in the "decline of life" at this time and has no opportunity to worship God among Gentiles.[101] For Gill, such a declaration contains "the words of Christ unto his father."[102] It is subtle at this point, but Gill's principle is that typological connection is sometimes, intentionally, lacking in order for readers to be signaled to look for a divine character, Jesus Christ.

Psalm 110

Psalm 110 is where Gill's need for a tool beyond typology in certain situations is drawn out more explicitly. Gill attributes the writing of this text to David, yet it could not be about him considering the subject's designation of divinity in verse 1. With the support of Tertullian and the authority of Christ and the apostles' citations of it (Matt 22:43, 44; Acts 2:34; 1 Cor 15:25; Heb 1:13), Gill attributes the psalm to the Messiah due to the character of David's lack of correlation with its divine attribute.[103] Another strike against linking David with Christ typologically is that David did not ascend to the heavens as the text indicates.[104] Gill then concludes that Ps 110 is "only applicable to Christ, and cannot be accommodated to any other; no, not to David as a type, as some psalms concerning him may."[105] In this case of divine characteristics, typology is unwarranted as a tool for bridging the Old Testament prophet with the New Testament reference. Moreover, the connection of the text with Christ is too direct for a typological reading to handle.[106]

With typology ruled out, Gill transitions directly to Father-Son discourse, as "these are the words of Jehovah the Father to his Son the Messiah."[107] Only the Son was "privy" to this decree of the Father spoken in eternity promising the Son his reward as mediatorial savior in the completion of his redemptive mission.[108] In line with Bates' attempt to legitimize the detection of divine persons interacting through the engaged in (Bates, *Birth of the Trinity*, 68–69).

101 Gill, *Exposition of the New Testament*, 2:572–3.

102 Gill, *Exposition of the New Testament*, 2:572–3. The same logic is applied by Gill in Pss 16 and 69 (see Gill, *Exposition of the Old Testament*, 3:582–3, 807).

103 Gill, *Exposition of the Old Testament*, 4:180–1.

104 Gill, *Body of Divinity*, 590–1.

105 Gill, *Exposition of the Old Testament*, 4:180–1. Gill believes that it is the conclusion of Peter in Acts 2:34–36 (see Gill, *Exposition of the New Testament*, 2:159).

106 Gill agrees with Bates' rejection of typology in Ps 110:1, since "the words spoken were not suitable for David qua David" (Bates, *Birth of the Trinity*, 161).

107 Gill, *Exposition of the Old Testament*, 4:181.

108 Gill, *Exposition of the Old Testament*, 4:181.

revelation of Old Testament prophetic texts, Gill makes a similar claim. He contends David, "under divine inspiration, had knowledge of the above divine transactions" in Ps 110.[109] For Gill, it produces a biblically warranted basis for Christ's pre-existence and prophesied mission as the mediatorial Prophet, Priest, and King.[110] In his comments on Christ's use of Ps 110:1 in Matt 22, where Jesus prods the Pharisees for making sense of the divine aspects of the character spoken to, Gill sees Christ invoking the same objection to designating David as the dialogue partner even if he wrote the psalm under divine inspiration.[111] Christ's questions provoke a revealing of the messianic hermeneutics. For Gill, "the question is to be answered upon true and just notions of the Messiah, but unanswerable upon the principles of the Pharisees."[112] It seems that Gill believes the ability of David to "personate" the Messiah and drop in on certain "divine transactions" is a part of Messianic understanding. PE is a necessary tool that fits better than typology for certain christological psalms and their interpretations in the New Testament.

Conclusion

The dichotomy between typology and PE in the current discussion, whether real or misunderstood, is a bottleneck for constructive dialogue between Bates' retrieval project and those holding to a traditional divinely-inspired-typological approach. Yet Gill breaks open the possibility of analyzing what PE looks like in the interpretation of a pre-critical, classical, Christocentric, and Reformed orthodox tradition. Gill cannot be accused of sacrificing typology for prosopological interpretation in his corpus. A perusal of his commentaries on any canonical book reveals typological connections on almost every page. Typology is his most frequently used tool in finding intertextual agreement, but it is not his only tool. PE is utilized in a multitude of prophetic passages alongside typological interpretation. In textual situations where the exegesis points to a disconnect between the prophetic subject and the characteristics designated to him, especially characteristics of divinity unique to the eternal Son, Gill takes typology off the table and opts for PE as a more suitable utensil for interpretation. Bates' simple formula, "if not the ancient prophet, then a theodramatic character," is an apt description of Gill's solution to the characters of Pss 2 and 110, and other texts, where Gill sees prophets "personate" Christ.[113]

As for critics who insist PE could not be the approach of the Old Testament prophets, Gill could say that these authors are more aware of the "spiritual sense" interpretations than the opponents are willing to concede, and the spiritual interpretation of these texts by the New Testament authors is sufficient for legitimizing it.[114] For Gill, PE and typology are what scripture interpreting scripture means for a Post-Reformation

---

109 Gill, *Body of Divinity*, 607–8.

110 Gill, *Body of Divinity*, 607–8.

111 Gill, *Body of Divinity*, 264–6.

112 John Gill, *An Exposition of the New Testament* (London: Mathews and Leigh, 1809), 1:265–6.

113 Bates, *Birth of the Trinity*, 182.

114 John Gill, *An Exposition of the Book of Solomon's Song; Commonly Called Canticles* (London: William Hill Collingridge, 1854), 4.

exegete. Though Gill's Christology and trinitarianism is not as tied to PE as Bates', PE plays an important role in allowing Gill to derive christological doctrines from texts like Pss 2 and 110.[115] In other words, Gill's classical Christology involves his prosopological interpretations. As for Bates' project, instead of seeing typology as a barrier to fruitful PE, Gill provides an overarching typological approach that incorporates PE when typology does not meet the demands of a Christocentric hermeneutic. Contrary to Bates, Gill is insistent on demonstrating typological correlation between Christ and the life of David in most of the Psalms. Exposing Gill's prosopological readings does not solve the need to discern PE's overall legitimacy, and Gill's interpretive moves themselves are not always precise.[116] Nevertheless, it provides a unique interlocutor to a debate stuck in patristics and modern biblical studies without many dialogue partners in the middle. Gill is evidence that PE is a legitimate part of pre-critical interpretation in the Post-Reformation era, and it is significant for Christocentric hermeneutics and formulations of Christology.

---

[115] For more on Gill's classical trinitarianism, see Steven Tshombe Godet, "The Trinitarian Theology of John Gill (1697–1771): Context, Sources, and Controversy" (PhD diss., The Southern Baptist Theological Seminary, 2015).

[116] I agree with Ortlund that at times Gill is unclear in differentiating prophetic interpretation and typological symbolism (see Ortlund, "John Gill as Interpreter," 107–8).

A devoted husband and sympathetic friend: The life and spirituality of Philip Doddridge

Zeyuan David Zhou

David Zhou is a Ph.D. student at the Southern Baptist Theological Seminary and an assistant pastor at Jarvis Street Baptist Church in Toronto.

Philip Doddridge (1702–1751), a prominent 18th-century Nonconformist pastor and theologian, articulated his integrative approach to life and spirituality through his poignant epigram:

> Live, while you live, the epicure would say,
> And seize the pleasures of the present day.
> Live, while you live, the sacred preacher cries,
> And give to God each moment as it flies.
> Lord, in my veins let both united be;
> I live in pleasure, when I live to thee.[1]

This epigram, considered as one of the finest in the English language, represents Doddridge's personal motto and reflects his philosophical commitment to reconciling temporal enjoyment with spiritual devotion. His life and work vividly demonstrate this synthesis, as he balanced his roles as a pastor, educator, and hymn-writer with his personal relationships and daily experiences. Doddridge's approach to living, as captured in his writing and correspondence, reveals a profound integration of pleasure and piety. As a devoted husband and sympathetic friend, he navigated both his public responsibilities and private life with a holistic view of spirituality. This article examines how Doddridge's philosophy of life—where pleasure and piety coexist—shaped his personal journey of faith, providing a compelling model of evangelical spirituality for Christians in every generation.

---

1 Ernest A. Payne, "Eighteenth Century English Congregationalism as Exemplified in the Life and Work of Philip Doddridge," *Review & Expositor* 48.3 (1951): 301.

Biographical Sketch of Philip Doddridge
Born in London on June 26, 1702, Doddridge was the twentieth child of a shopkeeper.[2] His family had deep Puritan and Reformation roots, with his paternal grandfather, John Doddridge, resigning as vicar of Shepperton-on-Thames due to the Act of Uniformity in 1662, and his maternal grandmother exiled from Bohemia in 1626 for supporting the Protestant church.[3] Following the deaths of his parents in 1711 and 1715, respectively, Doddridge found guidance and mentorship under Samuel Clarke (1675–1729), the minister at St. Albans.[4] Four years later, Doddridge moved to Kibworth Beauchamp, Leicestershire, where he continued his theological training under John Jennings (c.1687–1723), a respected minister who prepared Doddridge for a life of ministry.[5] At the age of eighteen, Doddridge was introduced to the works of John Locke (1632–1704), whose philosophy informed his rational approach to theology and his defense of Christianity.[6]

In 1723, at the age of twenty-one, Doddridge accepted his first pastoral charge at Kibworth after the Jennings' death.[7] In 1729, he moved to Northampton, where he founded and operated one of the largest and most successful Dissenting academies.[8] From 1730 to his death in 1751, Doddridge also served as the pastor of the Independent congregation at Castle Hill in Northampton.[9] The academy attracted a diverse body of students, including Baptists, Presbyterians, and Anglicans, many of whom went on to have successful careers in ministry and other secular fields.[10] Doddridge was among the first to introduce lecturing in English rather than Latin, and developed a system of shorthand for students to record lectures verbatim.[11] As a polymath, Doddridge's academic influence extended beyond theology to include mathematics, general physics, and natural philosophy, being well-versed especially in the works of Sir Isaac Newton (1643–1727).[12]

Four of Doddridge's works stand out as especially significant, earning him notable recognition during his lifetime.[13] The first was a threefold *Answer* (1742–1743), an

---

2 D.L. Jeffrey, "Doddridge, Philip," in *Biographical Dictionary of Evangelicals*, ed. Timothy Larsen, David Bebbington, and Mark A. Nolls (Downers Grove, IL: InterVarsity, 2003), 187.

3 Jeffrey, "Doddridge, Philip," 187.

4 Geoffrey F. Nuttall, "Doddridge, Philip," in *Dictionary of Evangelical Biography, 1730–1860*, ed. Donald M. Lewis (Peabody, MA: Hendrickson, 2004), 1:314.

5 Nuttall, "Doddridge, Philip," 1:314.

6 Jeffrey, "Doddridge, Philip," 187.

7 Nuttall, "Doddridge, Philip," 1:314.

8 Jeffrey, "Doddridge, Philip," 187.

9 Jeffrey, "Doddridge, Philip," 187.

10 Jeffrey, "Doddridge, Philip," 187.

11 Jeffrey, "Doddridge, Philip," 187.

12 Jeffrey, "Doddridge, Philip," 187.

13 Nuttall, "Doddridge, Philip," 1:315.

intellectual apologetic providing a rational defense of Christianity against the deists.[14] The second, which was perhaps Doddridge's most influential work, *The Rise and Progress of Religion in the Soul* (1745), which was considered by evangelicals, more than a century after its publication, as "the safest, completest, and most effectual manual for anxious enquirers' into Christianity."[15] Many were converted by reading this book, including the stateman and leading abolitionist William Wilberforce (1759–1833). The third work that brought Doddridge eminence was a *Life* (1747) of Colonel James Gardiner (1688–1745), presenting a Puritan hagiography that became influential in the evangelical revivals in the eighteenth century.[16] Fourth, what further cemented Doddridge's reputation was his *magnum opus*, *The Family Expositor* (5 vols, 1738–1756), a tome of biblical commentary that continued to be studied long after his death.[17] In addition, his *Course of Lectures* (1763), published posthumously, became a foundational text for theological education in many dissenting academies.[18] Today, however, it is perhaps through his hymns that Doddridge is most enduringly remembered.[19]

Under the nurture of his mother, Monica Bauman, Doddridge's personal life was marked by close relationships and a high regard for women.[20] Even after he left home, Doddridge continued to have an intimate connection with his mother. At the age of nineteen, confessing his growing desire for courting the opposite sex, Doddridge wrote: "But madam, I leave it entirely in your breast, and must only add, to prevent being mistaken, that though I am in so much haste for a mistress, I can stay seven years for a wife."[21] After corresponding with several young women, On December 22, 1730, at the age of twenty-eight, Doddridge married Mercy Maris (1709–1790), an orphan from Worcester.[22] Their marriage was noted for its godly character, intense affection, and sincere friendship.[23] Despite the challenges of pastoral and academic responsibilities, Doddridge maintained a lively and affectionate correspondence with friends and family, revealing his warm and engaging personality.[24] In his final years, Doddridge's health deteriorated due to tuberculosis. In the summer of 1751, Doddridge was persuaded to travel to Lisbon in the hope of recovery, but he succumbed to the disease on

---

14 Nuttall, "Doddridge, Philip," 1:315.

15 Jeffrey, "Doddridge," 187–8.

16 Nuttall, "Doddridge, Philip," 1:315.

17 Nuttall, "Doddridge, Philip," 1:315.

18 Nuttall, "Doddridge, Philip," 1:315.

19 For in-depth analysis on the hymns of Philip Doddridge, see Graham C. Ashworth, "Philip Doddridge (1702–1751): The Theology of His Hymns" (PhD diss., Trinity Theological Seminary, 2002); Robert Strivens, *Philip Doddridge and the Shaping of Evangelical Dissent* (Abingdon, Oxon: Routledge, 2016).

20 Jeffrey, "Doddridge, Philip," 188.

21 Jeffrey, "Doddridge, Philip," 188.

22 Jeffrey, "Doddridge, Philip," 188.

23 For a detailed account of their marriage, see Joseph C. Harrod, "A 'Happy Union': Piety in the Marriage of Philip and Mercy Doddridge," *Churchman* 129.2 (2015): 149–66.

24 Jeffrey, "Doddridge, Philip," 188.

October 26, 1751, leaving behind his wife, Mercy, and four of their nine children.[25]

A Devoted Husband: The Marriage of Philip Doddridge and Mercy Maris
On August 6, 1730, Doddridge wrote to Mrs. Owen, the great-aunt of Mercy Maris, requesting her permission to court the "bright jewel" he had encountered during his summer holiday in Worcester.[26] At the end of this letter, Doddridge expressed his desire to court Mercy and offered his perspective on the nature of Christian marriage:

> I have nothing further to add, but that, as it is my desire to be devoted to the service of my God, so I humbly defer this dear affair to the determination of his wise and gracious Providence. Agreeable and lovely as she is in all other respects, I hope I should never have thought of her as a wife, if I had not found reason to believe that she was truly religious. And as the hope of our being companions and helpmates in the way to heaven, would add the greatest relish to my union with her, so the prospect of meeting her at the end of our pilgrimage, and spending an eternity with her, in a nobler state of existence, would, I trust, be one means of composing my mind, if God should deny me so desirable a blessing. In the mean time, madam, I promise myself the kindest offices from your friendship, which are consistent with your regard to her; and hope, that if her relatives do not think fit to accept of his proposal, they will at least forgive it.[27]

The above passage reveals that Doddridge viewed Christian marriage as a deeply spiritual union, grounded in mutual faith and devotion to God. He expresses a desire for marriage that goes beyond mere companionship or affection, emphasizing the importance of shared religious convictions. Doddridge considers his potential wife's piety as a crucial factor in his decision to marry, indicating that spiritual union is essential for a successful and happy marriage. In addition, Doddridge depicts marriage as a partnership in the Christian journey, where spouses serve as "companions and helpmates in the way to heaven."[28] Such a metaphor suggests that he saw marriage as a means of mutual support, helping each other grow in faith and ultimately reaching the heavenly destiny. The idea of spending "an eternity with her, in a nobler state of existence" indicates that Doddridge viewed marriage as not only a temporal arrangement but also as having eternal significance.[29] As Joseph C. Harrod remarks, "God was part of their everyday experiences of life, be it as mundane as a travel narrative or as dangerous as the threat of illness to their children. Piety was part of the warp and woof of their daily

---

25 Jeffrey, "Doddridge, Philip," 188. After Philip Doddridge's death, Mrs. Doddridge remained a widow for forty years and died at the age of eighty-two.

26 John Doddridge Humphreys, ed., *The Correspondence and Diary of Philip Doddridge, D.D. Illustrative of Various Particulars in his Life hitherto Unknown: with Many Notices of his Contemporaries; and a Sketch of the Ecclesiastical History of the Times in which he Lived* (London: Henry Colburn and Richard Bentley, 1830), 3:29.

27 Humphreys, *Correspondence and Diary of Philip Doddridge*, 3:33.

28 Humphreys, *Correspondence and Diary of Philip Doddridge*, 3:33.

29 Humphreys, *Correspondence and Diary of Philip Doddridge*, 3:33.

lives."³⁰

Doddridge's letters illustrate that his affection for Mercy was not merely superficial or driven by physical attraction but deeply rooted in her spiritual virtues. On August 30, 1730, he wrote to his friend Hannah Clark and praised Mercy's character: "In her, Cordelia, the domestic virtues of modesty, prudence, industry, and tenderness, guarded and consecrated by serious piety, are joined; with a degree of wit, beauty, and politeness, which, I fear, would have ensnared me, if it had appeared alone, and on so impressible a heart have made a speedy, if not a lasting conquest."³¹ The frequent and affectionate correspondence between Doddridge and Mercy during their courtship reveals the intensity of his feelings. From October 2 and December 6, 1730, Doddridge wrote to Mercy ten times, expressing the joy at the prospect of seeing her: "I hope, however, to see you once next week, if possible! and words cannot express the impatience with which I expect this delightful interview."³² After their meeting, Doddridge's heart was filled with tender satisfaction at Mercy's acceptance of his address: "Had I the most ample time, all I could say would be utterly insufficient to express the sense I entertain of your worth, and the warmth of my gratitude for the obliging reception you gave me. Words cannot express it; but my heart feels it so tenderly, that it often throbs with joy and fondness."³³

Doddridge also kept a healthy fear that his love for Mercy might rise to the level of idolatry and sought to keep God at the center of his affections. He expressed hope that Mercy would guide him towards God, acknowledging that it was God and His providence that brought them together and bestowed upon them the virtues and blessings they enjoyed:

> I fear I shall overlove you; and then perhaps God will afflict you. That is the only way in which I can fear being afflicted in you; as we must be in every thing which we suffer to usurp the place of God in our hearts. But I hope you will rather lead me to Him. I am sure it ought to be so; for I am fully conscious that it was He, that gave you that lovely form, that intelligence, that wisdom, generosity, and goodness ... it was He, that opened to me a heart which the greatest and best of men could hardly have deserved; and kindly disposed events, by His Providence, in a manner favorable to my dearest wishes. And is He to be forgotten and neglected in, and for this? No, my dearest, it shall not be.³⁴

His conscience would also reproach him if his love for Mercy were not in harmony with the solemn commitments surrounding the Lord's Supper. On November 1, 1730, Doddridge wrote:

> I am but just now risen from the table of the Lord, and I am sitting down to

---

30 Harrod, "A 'Happy Union,'" 154.

31 Humphreys, *Correspondence and Diary of Philip Doddridge*, 3:35.

32 Humphreys, *Correspondence and Diary of Philip Doddridge*, 3:44.

33 Humphreys, *Correspondence and Diary of Philip Doddridge*, 3:46.

34 Humphreys, *Correspondence and Diary of Philip Doddridge*, 3:46–47.

write to you. Nor does my conscience accuse me for such a transition. It would rather reproach me, if I had fixed my affections upon a lady with whom I could not correspond in a strain agreeably to the solemnity of such an hour. I am remembering a dying Redeemer, and I have been remembering you, who, I can truly say, hold the next place in my heart. May it ever be only the next![35]

Despite his deep affection for Mercy, Doddridge was careful to ensure that this love remained subordinate to his love for Christ. By stating that Mercy holds "the next place in my heart," he emphasizes that while she is cherished, his primary devotion remains with God.[36] This order of affection is something he prays will continue throughout their marriage. Yet simultaneously, this hierarchy of affection indicates that, in terms of human love, Mercy occupies the most significant place in his heart. After thirteen years of marriage, there was no indication that Doddridge's love for Mercy had diminished: "If hope if any memoirs of my life be ever written, the world will be informed of that most happy part of my history which relates to your character and affection, and takes its date from December 22, 1730."[37]

The strength of their marital bond would soon be tested by the fragility of life characteristic of the eighteenth century. The Doddridges were married in late December 1730, and by early October 1731, their first child, Elisabeth (also known as "Betsy" or "Testsy"), was born. Tragically, little Tetsy caught tuberculosis in June 1736 and passed away just days before her fifth birthday, leaving her parents devastated by grief.[38] In 1733, they welcomed Mary (later known as "Polly"), followed by Mercy (1734–1809), Philip (1735–1785), and Anna Cecilia ("Caecilia") (1737–1811). Between 1739 and 1748, the family experienced the sorrow of losing four more children: Samuel (1739–1740), twin daughters Sarah and Jane (1746, who lived only two days), and William (1748, who survived for six days).[39] By 1740, having already buried two of their children, several of their other children fell ill during August and September of that year, with Mercy away in London, and it is not surprise that their correspondence was filled with fervent prayers during those challenging days.

On August 15, 1740, Doddridge wrote to his wife, informing her that their youngest daughter, Cecilia, was gravely ill.[40] He expressed his fear that their situation was dire and implored her to continue praying earnestly, while also submitting to the divine will. By the following day, he updated her with a slightly more hopeful report: Cecilia's condition had improved significantly, and their son Philip was not as ill as initially feared.[41] But a few days later, Cecilia's condition had worsened, placing her in consid-

---

35 Humphreys, *Correspondence and Diary of Philip Doddridge*, 3:50–51.

36 Humphreys, *Correspondence and Diary of Philip Doddridge*, 3:50–51.

37 Humphreys, *Correspondence and Diary of Philip Doddridge*, 4:172.

38 Harrod, "A 'Happy Union,'" 157. Philip Doddridge preached his daughter's funeral sermon, later published as *Submission to Divine Providence* the following year.

39 Harrod, "A 'Happy Union,'" 157. The Doddridges also suffered several miscarriages and early births during these years.

40 Humphreys, *Correspondence and Diary of Philip Doddridge*, 3:490.

41 Humphreys, *Correspondence and Diary of Philip Doddridge*, 3:491.

erable danger. Despite the dire situation, Doddridge maintained hope and confidence in God's care:

> The children are recovering … But none of our earthly joys are unmixed: this morning, just before prayer, I received an account of dear Caecilia's being much worse, and in considerable danger! She is yet within the reach of prayer, and I am not without hope; but the symptoms are undoubtedly dangerous; and if she lives she is, as I greatly hope she will be, given to prayer. I bless God amidst this surprise, I am calm—confident in his care, and rejoicing exceedingly in his love. I know he will be with you and bless you![42]

Mercy, reflecting on the situation, conveyed great distress and struggled with prayer and submission to God's will:

> I desire to own with thankfulness his goodness to us in supporting our minds under the trial: though I confess this evening I find my mind so uncertain how it may have pleased an all-wise and good God, to have determined with regard to dear Caecilia, and so impressed with the extremity of her case, that I scarcely know what to write, nor how to pray for her; to-morrow I expect will determine it—and I desire to be brought to an entire submission to the Divine will; however the event may be, I know it is wise and good.[43]

Ultimately, Cecilia's survival was a source of immense joy and gratitude for the distressed mother. She wrote to her husband Philip: "I desire to join with you in returning our united thanks to the Divine Author of all our mercies, for his great goodness to our dear children; for surely we have abundant reason for thankfulness that ours are spared to us, whilst infinite Wisdom is making breaches upon so many of our friends around us."[44] Then, she praised God in a pious resolve: "May we remember by whose power it is that 'our mountain stand strong;' and may our hearts be duly disposed to render to Him the daily tributes of praise, love, and obedience, for all his mercies to us and ours."[45]

A Sympathetic Friend: Doddridge's Reception of George Whitefield
The extent of Doddridge's engagement with various Christian denominations, including Baptists, Moravians, Anglicans, and Methodists, reveal his commitment to fostering a sympathetic understanding across diverse theological perspectives.[46] Although this was sometimes challenging, few in the early eighteenth century were as broadly

---

[42] Humphreys, *Correspondence and Diary of Philip Doddridge*, 3:496.

[43] Humphreys, *Correspondence and Diary of Philip Doddridge*, 3:497–8.

[44] Humphreys, *Correspondence and Diary of Philip Doddridge*, 3:507.

[45] Humphreys, *Correspondence and Diary of Philip Doddridge*, 3:507.

[46] For a more thorough discussion on Doddridge's relationships with these Christian denominations, see F.W. Harris, "Philip Doddridge: Eighteenth-Century Ecumenist," *Foundations* 14.3 (1971): 251–70.

informed and interested in the global state of the church as Doddridge. His broad interests and inclusive perspective connected him with a diverse array of individuals.[47] Doddridge also maintained a keen interest in the religious revival in New England, notably under the leadership of Jonathan Edwards (1703–1758), receiving periodic updates about its progress.[48] Doddridge's connections with other denominations were likely far greater in scope than those of most independent ministers of his time. While his broad and inclusive approach sometimes drew criticism, it also contributed to a more tolerant and empathetic atmosphere among Christians of different traditions.[49]

Among Doddridge's extensive correspondences, his engagement with George Whitefield (1714–1770) particularly reveals the significant difference between his own open-minded perspective and the narrower outlook of most Dissenters at that time. In May, 1739, Whitefield visited Northampton and wrote in his journal that he was "most courteously received by Dr. Doddridge, master of the academy there."[50] He also recorded that he preached there at seven to an audience of approximately three thousand on a common near the town and delivered another sermon the following morning at around eight.[51] Initially, Doddridge balanced his reception of Whitefield with a sense of caution and criticized him in a letter to Nathaniel Wood, Doddridge's former tutor at St. Alban's, on September 10, 1741: "I am sorry to hear Mr. Whitfield has misrepresented things, as your letter imports, I take him to be a very honest, though a very weak man. Who can wonder if so much popularity has a little intoxicated him? He certainly does much good, and I am afraid some harm."[52] In July, 1743, Doddridge displayed enough boldness to participate in services at Whitefield's tabernacle, which prompted a stern warning from Isaac Watts (1674–1748): "I am sorry that since your departure I have had many questions asked me about your preaching or praying at the Tabernacle, and sinking the character of a Minister, and especially of a Tutor, among the dissenters so low thereby. I find many of your friends entertain this idea; but I can give no answer, as not knowing how much you have been engaged there. I pray God to guard us from every temptation."[53] Despite this caution, Doddridge took an even more controversial step later that year by allowing Whitefield to preach in his Northampton pulpit. This decision quickly became known in London and beyond, leading to further concerns.[54] On October 11, 1743, Nathaniel Neal (d. 1769) wrote to Doddridge:

---

47 Within the Church of England alone, Doddridge's circle of correspondence included some of the most important dignitaries: "Dr. Thomas Sherlock, Bishop of London, (1678–1761), Dr. Tucker, Dean of Gloucester, (1712–1799), Dr. Thomas Herring, Archbishop of Canterbury, (1693–1757), Dr. Secker, Bishop of Oxford, (1693–1768), Dr. Isaac Maddox, Bishop of Worcester, (1697–1759), and Dr. William Warburton (1698–1779), who became Bishop of Gloucester several years after Doddridge's death" (Harris, "Philip Doddridge: Eighteenth-Century Ecumenist," 256).

48 Harris, "Philip Doddridge," 268.

49 Harris, "Philip Doddridge," 269.

50 A.G. Secrett, "Philip Doddridge and the Evangelical Revival in the Eighteenth Century," *Evangelical Quarterly* 23.4 (1951): 252.

51 Harris, "Philip Doddridge," 266.

52 Humphreys, *Correspondence and Diary of Philip Doddridge*, 4:56.

53 Humphreys, *Correspondence and Diary of Philip Doddridge*, 4:269.

54 Harris, "Philip Doddridge," 267.

It was with the utmost concern that I received the information of Mr. Whitefield's having preached last week in your pulpit, and that I attended the meeting of the trustees (i.e., the trustees of the Academy, the Coward Trust) this day, when that matter was canvassed, and that I now find myself obliged to apprise you of the very great uneasiness which your conduct herein has occasioned them … For my own part, I have had the misfortune of observing, and I must not conceal it from you, that wherever I have heard it mentioned that Dr. Doddridge countenanced the methodists, and it has been the subject of conversation much oftener than I could have wished, I have heard it constantly spoken of by his friends with concern, as threatening a great diminution of his usefulness, and by his adversaries with a sneer of triumph.[55]

In a later correspondence, Doddridge replied to Nathaniel with a sense of regret that Whitefield had arrived in Northampton at such an inopportune time and confided with him the true reason behind the accusation:

I must, indeed, look upon it as an unhappy circumstance that he came to Northampton just when he did, as I perceive, that in concurrence with other circumstances, it has filled town and country with astonishment and indignation. Nor did I, indeed, imagine my character to have been of such great importance in the world, as that this little incident should have been taken so much notice of. I believe the true reason is, that for no other fault than my not being able to go so far as some of my brethren into the new ways of thinking and speaking, I have long had a multitude of enemies, who have been watching for some occasion against me; and I thank God that they have hitherto, with all that malignity of heart which some of them have expressed, been able to find no greater![56]

Doddridge's openness to engaging with "enthusiasts" beyond his dissenting tradition appears to stem from two main factors: his contemporary theological perspective and his commitment to revival and mission. Richard A. Muller observes that Doddridge's rationalistic and scientific approach to theology "arguably led him away from an assertive or polemical approach and led some of his students toward more heterodox formulations."[57] Moreover, the structure and sequence of his lectures reflect Doddridge's dedication to reconciling reason and faith, but this arrangement also signifies a departure from the traditional ordering found in older orthodox Reformed theologies, such as those by Friedrich Spanheim (1632–1701) and Francis Turretin (1623–1687).[58] In an age when Christian Aristotelianism and traditional substance metaphysics were being replaced by new rationalisms—particularly mechanical and

---

55 Harris, "Philip Doddridge," 274.

56 Humphreys, *Correspondence and Diary of Philip Doddridge*, 4:290–1.

57 Richard A. Muller, "Philip Doddridge and the Formulation of Calvinistic Theology in an Era of Rationalism and Deconfessionalization," in *Religion, Politics, and Dissent: 1660-1832, Essays in Honour of James E. Bradley*, ed. Robert D. Cornwall and William Gibson (Aldershot, Hampshire: Ashgate, 2010), 72.

58 Muller, "Philip Doddridge and the Formulation of Calvinistic Theology," 72.

mathematical philosophies—and when theology faced the choice of either integrating these principles as foundational assumptions or resorting to increasingly vague reiterations of outdated principles, Doddridge opted for adaptation.[59] As Doddridge chose to engage the rational philosophies of his era, he developed a theology that was notably more rationalistic compared to the orthodox positions of the seventeenth century.[60] Thus, as Roger Thomas aptly concludes, Doddridge's theological position was a "moderate orthodoxy" in which "the moderation consists not so much in a reduced orthodoxy as in a reduced dogmatism."[61]

Another factor that made Doddridge more inclined to embrace the Methodists in a friendly and cooperative manner was his vision for spiritual revival. F.W. Harris observed, "No one was more concerned about the revival of religion than Doddridge, and he was able to recognize that, in spite of their faults, the Methodists too were most anxious about it, and were actually engaged upon the work of revival."[62] Although Doddridge himself could never have been accused of being an "enthusiast," he was nevertheless a minister of the Gospel of Jesus Christ, a calling which he considered "the most desirable employment in the world."[63] It was Geoffrey Nuttall (1911–2007) who also observed that evangelism was "the thread on which his multi-colored life was strung. It was for this above all that he wrote, preached, corresponded and educated his students in the Academy."[64] For Doddridge, the message of the cross was both the content of and impetus for revival. In his sermon *Christ's Invitation to Thirsty Souls*, he proclaims:

> View him, my brethren, not only in the precious scenes of his abasement, his descent from heaven, and his abode on earth; but view him on mount Calvary, extended on the cross, torn with thorns, wounded with nails, pierced with a spear; and then say, whether there be not a voice in each of these sacred wounds, which loudly proclaims the tenderness of his heart, and demonstrates, beyond all possibility of dispute or suspicion, his readiness to relieve the distressed soul,

---

59 Muller, "Philip Doddridge and the Formulation of Calvinistic Theology," 72.

60 For a summary of Doddridge's theology of revelation, sin, human freedom, predestination, and divine sovereignty, see Muller, "Philip Doddridge and the Formulation of Calvinistic Theology," 74–82.

61 Roger Thomas, "Philip Doddridge and Liberalism in Religion," in *Philip Doddridge, 1702-51: His Contribution to English Religion*, ed. Geoffrey F. Nuttall (London: Independent Press, 1951), 134. Robert Striven has criticized Doddridge for his unassertive and somewhat weak stance regarding doctrine and theology: "Doddridge, it is suggested, failed to hold sufficiently tightly to the prime importance which the Puritans placed upon doctrine and theology. He loosened the close link which they maintained between a person's doctrinal beliefs and his experience of God. He failed to see the need to defend foundational doctrines, such as the Trinity, and in that area and others sought to give Christian love and fellowship a higher place in his thinking, teaching and practice than biblical doctrine. As a result, Doddridge, no doubt unwittingly, played some part in the doctrinal downgrade which so sadly mars the experience of much of eighteenth-century English Dissent" (Robert Strivens, "Evangelical Spirituality in Eighteenth-Century Dissent: Philip Doddridge and John Gill," *Foundations* 65 [2013]: 19).

62 Harris, "Philip Doddridge," 268.

63 Alan C. Clifford, "The Christian Mind of Philip Doddridge (1702–1751): The Gospel According to an Evangelical Congregationalist," *Evangelical Quarterly* 56 (1984): 227.

64 Clifford, "The Christian Mind of Philip Doddridge," 228.

that cries to him for the blessings of the gospel.[65]

Conclusion

The life and scholarship of Philip Doddridge exemplify a profound synthesis of temporal enjoyment and spiritual devotion, embodying the ethos of his memorable epigram. His ability to integrate pleasure with piety reflects a holistic approach to evangelical spirituality, one that transcends mere intellectual engagement to embrace the full spectrum of human experience. Doddridge's marriage to Mercy Maris, characterized by shared faith and deep affection, underscores his belief in the sanctity of marriage as a spiritual companionship. His charitable attitude toward diverse Christian traditions, including his interaction with George Whitefield, illustrates his commitment to fostering unity and understanding across denominational boundaries. Through his prolific writings and educational endeavors, Doddridge demonstrates that rigorous intellectual inquiry and heartfelt spiritual devotion are not mutually exclusive but rather complementary. His life, marked by resilience amid personal and ministerial challenges, offers a compelling model of how to navigate between temporal and eternal concerns. As such, Doddridge's legacy continues to inspire, providing enduring insights into the integration of faith with everyday life and serving as a guiding example for contemporary and future generations of Christians.

---

65 Clifford, "The Christian Mind of Philip Doddridge," 233.

Pastoral usefulness: retrieving wisdom from the letters of Benjamin Beddome[1]

Yuta Seki

Yuta Seki is the Senior Pastor of Maple Avenue Baptist Church in Georgetown, Ontario, and a DEdMin student at The Southern Baptist Theological Seminary. His doctoral thesis is on the pastoral theology of Benjamin Beddome, and his research interests are eighteenth-century English Particular Baptists and Baptists in Ontario and Canada.

Benjamin Beddome (1718–1795) was the pastor of the Baptist church in Bourton-on-the-Water in south central England.[2] On one occasion, Beddome found himself at a

[1] This article was presented at the annual meeting of the Evangelical Theological Society Ontario & Quebec, Toronto, ON, October 12, 2024.The article is also an adaptation from a chapter in Yuta Seki, "'Long May Thy Servant Feed Thy Sheep': Pastoral Ministry in the Life and Thought of Benjamin Beddome," DEdMin thesis, The Southern Baptist Theological Seminary, 2025. The thesis will be published as Yuta Seki, *Long May Thy Servant Feed Thy Sheep: The Pastoral Theology of Benjamin Beddome* (Eugene, OR: Pickwick, 2025).

[2] For sources on Beddome, see Anonymous, "Memoir," in *Sermons Printed from the Manuscripts of the Late Rev. Benjamin Beddome, A.M. of Bourton-on-the-Water, Gloucestershire*, by Benjamin Beddome (London: William Ball, 1835), ix–xxviii; Thomas Brooks, *Pictures of the Past: The History of the Baptist Church, Bourton-on-the-Water* (London: Judd & Glass, 1861), 21–66; Kenneth Dix, "'Thy Will Be Done': A Study in the Life of Benjamin Beddome," *Bulletin of the Strict Baptist Historical Society* 9 (1972): n.p.; Roger Hayden, *Continuity and Change: Evangelical Calvinism Among Eighteenth-Century Baptist Ministers Trained at Bristol Academy, 1690–1791* (Chipping Norton, UK: Nigel Lynn, 2006), 80–91, 154–8, 168–72; Michael A. G. Haykin, "Benjamin Beddome (1717–1795)," in *The British Particular Baptists, 1638–1910*, ed. Michael A. G. Haykin and Terry Wolever (Springfield, MO: Particular Baptist Press, 2018), 4:258–73; Michael A. G. Haykin, Roy M. Paul, and Jeongmo Yoo, eds., *Glory to the Three Eternal: Tercentennial Essays on the Life and Writings of Benjamin Beddome (1718–1795)*, Monographs in Baptist History 13 (Eugene, OR: Pickwick, 2019); Derrick Holmes, "The Early Years (1655–1740) of Bourton-on-the-Water Dissenters Who Later Constituted the Baptist Church, with Special Reference to the Ministry of the Reverend Benjamin Beddome A.M. 1740–1795" (Cheltenham, Unpublished Certificate in Education Dissertation, St. Paul's College, 1969); Jason C. Montgomery, "Benjamin Beddome: The Fruitful Life and Evangelical Labor of a Forgotten Village Preacher" (PhD diss., Southwestern Baptist Theological Seminary, 2018); Stephen Pickles, *Cotswolds Pastor and Baptist Hymn Writer: The Life and Times of Benjamin Beddome* (Upham, UK: James Bourne Society, 2023); Daniel S. Ramsey, "'The Blessed Spirit': An Analysis of the Pneumatology of Benjamin Bed-

meeting of ministers in the nearby town of Fairford, Gloucestershire. Beddome was scheduled to preach, but when the service began, he forgot what he had intended to say. Since he did not preach from notes, he could not consult them. Instead, he asked the host pastor, Thomas Davis (d. 1784), "Brother Davis, what must I preach from?" Taken back by Beddome's question, Davis replied, "Ask no foolish questions." The Bourton pastor was relieved and took Titus 3:9 as his text, "Avoid foolish questions" and, according to Beddome's first biographer, John Rippon (1751–1836), "preached a remarkably methodical, correct, and useful discourse on it."[3] Evidently, Beddome was capable in the pulpit. Rippon remarked of Beddome's preaching: "He fed [his people] with the finest of the wheat. No man in all his connexions wrote more sermons, nor composed them with greater care—and this was true of him to the last weeks of his life."[4]

The Bourton pastor was respected in the Midland Association and amongst the English Particular Baptists.[5] He produced *A Scriptural Exposition of the Baptist Catechism* which was widely used in his denomination and at their training center, the Bristol Baptist Academy.[6] Through the posthumous publication of his sermons and

---

dome as an Early Evangelical" (PhD diss., The Southern Baptist Theological Seminary, 2017); John Rippon, "Rev. Benjamin Beddome, A. M. Bourton-on-the-Water, Gloucestershire," in *The Baptist Annual Register, for 1794, 1795, 1796-1797* (London, 1797), 314–26. Hereafter, Brooks, *Pictures of the Past* will be abbreviated to Brooks, *POTP*.

3 Rippon, "Rev. Benjamin Beddome," 321. The anecdote and the sermon were published as John Rippon, "Sketch of a Sermon by the Late Rev. B. Beddome," in *Baptist Annual Register for 1798, 1799, 1800, and Part of 1801* (London, 1801), 415–21. The sermon was also published as Benjamin Beddome, "Sermon 10," in *Twenty Short Discourses, Adapted to Village Worship or the Devotions of the Family* (London: W. Simpkin and R. Marshall, 1833), 5:81–89. Haykin recounts these events as an example of how "many of the best preachers of this community [the English Particular Baptists of the long eighteenth century] were, of course, able to preach with little preparation, if the need arose." Michael A. G. Haykin, "'Those Who Plead for Thee': English Particular Baptist Preaching in the Long Eighteenth Century," *Evangelical Quarterly* 94, no. 4 (December 2023): 3–5.

4 Rippon, "Rev. Benjamin Beddome," 320. In his day, Robert Hall Jr. (1764-1831) "was renowned as one of the most eloquent preachers of Great Britain." Michael A. G. Haykin, "Robert Hall, Sr. (1728–1791)," in *The British Particular Baptists, 1638-1910*, ed. Michael A. G. Haykin and Terry Wolever (Springfield, MO: Particular Baptist Press, 2019), 5:55; Cody H. McNutt adds, "He was one of the most celebrated figures among the Baptists of the Regency era, yet his fame extended far beyond Baptist circles." Cody Heath McNutt, "The Ministry of Robert Hall, Jr.: The Preacher as Theological Exemplar and Cultural Celebrity" (PhD diss., The Southern Baptist Theological Seminary, 2012), 2. Hall published a volume of Beddome's hymns in 1818 and said in the preface, "As a Preacher, he was universally admired for the piety and unction of his sentiments, the felicity of his arrangement, and the purity, force, and simplicity of his language; all which were recommended by a delivery perfectly natural and graceful." Robert Hall, ed., "Recommendatory Preface," in *Hymns Adapted to Public Worship, or Family Devotion: Now First Published, from the Manuscripts of the Late Rev. B. Beddome, A. M.*, by Benjamin Beddome (London, 1818), v–vi.

5 Rippon wrote, "How acceptable his labours were to the churches, when he could be prevailed on to visit them, has long been known at Abingdon, Bristol, London, and in the circle of the Midland Association." Rippon, "Rev. Benjamin Beddome," 322.

6 For a modern reprint of this catechism, see Benjamin Beddome, *A Scriptural Exposition of the Baptist Catechism* (1776; repr., Birmingham, AL: Solid Ground Christian Books, 2006). Haykin says, "The Bristol Baptist Academy [was] the sole British Baptist seminary for much of the eighteenth century." Michael A. G. Haykin, "'Glory to the Three Eternal': Benjamin Beddome and the Teaching of Trinitarian Theology in the

hymns, Beddome's legacy continued into the nineteenth century.[7] There are extant 225 sermons and 830 hymns, but this article will focus on a collection of Beddome's letters.

The letters were exchanged between the Baptist churches of Bourton-on-the-Water and Goodman's Fields in London. The latter was called the Little Prescott Street church and had recently lost its pastor, Samuel Wilson (1702–1750).[8] The deacons of the church searched for a replacement and requested that Beddome relocate to Goodman's Fields. The London church was familiar with Beddome since, a decade earlier, he was baptized and joined as a member.[9] The church now found itself inviting a former member to be their new pastor. As for Beddome, the invitation presented the opportunity to minister at a more significant church and have a wider influence. There were seven letters exchanged between Bourton and London between November 1750 and February 1751; to their analysis, we now turn.[10]

Eighteenth Century," *Southern Baptist Journal of Theology* 10, no. 1 (Spring 2006): 77. For the history and impact of the Bristol Academy, see David W. Bebbington, "The Significance of Bristol Baptist College," *Baptist Quarterly* 53, no. 4 (October 2022): 149–66; John Rippon, *A Brief Essay towards an History of the Baptist Academy at Bristol* (London, 1796); Jeongmo Yoo, "The Bristol Academy and the Education of Ministers in Eighteenth-Century England (1758–1791)," in *Church and School in Early Modern Protestantism: Studies in Honor of Richard A. Muller on the Maturation of a Theological Tradition*, ed. Jordan J. Ballor, David S. Sytsma, and Jason Zuidema, Studies in the History of Christian Traditions 170 (Leiden: Brill, 2013). The institution has been variably titled during its existence. For the first fifty years (1720–70), the school was referred to as an academy, but with the formation of the Bristol Education Society in 1770, the title "Seminary" was used. By 1812, the school was regularly called Bristol Baptist Academy, and in 1841, the printed annual reports called it, Bristol Baptist College. Roger Hayden, "Bristol Baptist Academy, 1720 to present," *Dissenting Academies Online: Database and Encyclopedia* (Dr Williams's Centre for Dissenting Studies, August 2011).

7 For a list of the primary sources primary and secondary sources on Beddome, see Yuta Seki, "A Resurgence of Benjamin Beddome Studies: A Bibliographic Essay," *Journal of Andrew Fuller Studies*, no. 8 (Spring 2024): 45–60.

8 For a history of the Little Prescott Street church from 1730–1768, see Joseph Ivimey, *A History of the English Baptists Comprising the Principal Events of the History of Protestant Dissenters, from the Revolution in 1668 till 1760; and of the London Baptist Churches, during That Period* (London: B. J. Holdworth. 1823), 3:542–61.

For sources on Wilson, see Anonymous, "Memoir of the Rev. Samuel Wilson," *The Baptist Magazine* 11 (April 1819): 141–45; John Gill, "Sermon [. . .] Occasioned by the Death of the Reverend Mr Samuel Wilson," in *A Collection of Sermons and Tracts* (London: George Keith, 1773); 1:477–98; Joseph Stennett, "A Funeral Sermon, at the Internment of the Reverend Mr. Samuel Wilson, in the Burial-Ground at Bunhill, October 12, 1750," in *Sermons on Various Subjects and Occasions*, by Samuel Wilson (London: G. Keith; J. Ward, 1753), 1–14.

9 For the sake of clarity, the reader should be aware that the phrases Little Prescott Street church, Goodman's Fields church, and London church will be used interchangeably.

10 These letters have appeared in several locations: Thomas Brooks, "Ministerial Changes a Hundred Years Ago," *Baptist Magazine* 51 (July 1859): 425–29; Thomas Brooks, "Ministerial Changes a Hundred Years Ago," *Baptist Magazine* 51 (August 1859): 482–87; Brooks, *POTP*, 32–47; Dix, "Thy Will Be Done," n.p.; Hayden, *Continuity and Change*, 82–86; Pickles, *Cotswolds Pastor*, 63–70. The version in Brooks, *Pictures of the Past* has the fullest information and is the version cited in this article.

Letters 1 and 2: Goodman's Fields to Bourton
At a meeting of the Little Prescott Street church on November 11, 1750, five deacons and thirty members signed and sent two letters to Bourton-on-the-Water.[11] In the first letter, the Goodman's Fields church requested for Beddome to relocate to London, considering the recent loss of their pastor.[12] If Beddome would come, they promised to love and respect him as a minister of the gospel.[13] The deacons appealed on the grounds of usefulness by drawing upon the Matthean parable of the talents (Matt 25:14–30).[14] Given they considered Beddome to have five talents, it was clear they thought much of Beddome's gifting and abilities.

The second letter from Goodman's Fields was addressed to the Bourton church and outlined the reasons why Beddome should remove to London.[15] Though they were reticent to call a pastor from the country, they had seen it done successfully by all three denominations in the city. They claimed their request was based solely upon necessity as there was no suitable replacement for Wilson. Given the declining state of the church in the city and the careless profession of many Christians, they needed someone of Beddome's caliber. Amongst Baptists, "learned" ministers were scarce, and so Goodman's Fields felt compelled to request for Beddome's removal.[16]

11 Goodman's Fields Church to Benjamin Beddome, November 11, 1750, in Brooks, *POTP*, 33.

12 Goodman's Fields Church to Benjamin Beddome, November 11, 1750, in Brooks, *POTP*, 32–33. To avoid excessive footnotes, the letter will be cited at its first mention. Thereafter, only direct quotes will be cited.

13 The duties of churches were set forth in the ordination sermons of English Particular Baptist pastors in the eighteenth century. At the ordination of George Braithwaite to the pastorate of Devonshire Square, London, on March 28, 1734, Wilson preached to the church regarding their duties. Ivimey, *History of the English Baptists*, 3:355. Wilson exhorted the church to have honorable thoughts of their pastor, converse with him respectfully, speak about him with affection and esteem, pray for their pastor, not receive an accusing report against him, follow their minister as he followed Christ, and provide for him cheerfully and generously. John Gill and Samuel Wilson, *The Mutual Duty of Pastor and People, Represented in Two Discourses Preached at the Ordination of the Reverend George Braithwaite, M. A.* (London: Aaron Ward, 1734), 4–27. Thus, the London church echoed the instructions of their former pastor, saying that they would act properly towards Beddome if he would come and be their pastor.

14 As will be demonstrated, usefulness was a prominent theme in the letters between Bourton and London. Beddome himself agreed that Christians should steward their talents according to their ability. In his sermon, "Motives to Usefulness," Beddome preached that Christians "should not be remiss and negligent, but exert themselves to the utmost in the service, and for the honour of their blessed Redeemer." He added while God generally chose lowly persons to be part of his kingdom, he sometimes plucked those "whose intellectual powers fit him for a large sphere of usefulness. Now, where much is given, much is required: a greater improvement is expected from the man who has five talents, than from him who is possessed of two." Beddome here quoted the same passage as the London deacons did in their letter. He continued, describing the kind of talents he had in mind: "A clear understanding, penetrating judgment, lively imagination, strong memory, and the like, are given to men to profit withal; and the service they perform should certainly be proportioned to their superior abilities." Benjamin Beddome, "Motives to Usefulness," in *Twenty Short Discourses, Adapted to Village Worship or the Devotions of the Family*, 2nd ed. (Dunstable, UK: J. W. Morris, 1807), 1:88–89. Thus, Beddome agreed with the London deacons that Christians and ministers should strive for greater usefulness.

15 Goodman's Fields Church to Bourton Church, November 11, 1750, in Brooks, *POTP*, 33–34.

16 The deacons of the London church lamented the scarcity of qualified ministers in the city, especially when "compared with the other two denominations," a reference to the Congregationalists and Presbyte-

The deacons were concerned if Beddome did not come, the people would disperse and the congregation dissolve, like the Joiners' Hall church recently under the care of Clendon Dawkes (d. 1758).¹⁷ The deacons concluded by mentioning the presence of a suitable replacement for Beddome amongst the Bourton membership and described the potential relocation to London as being "to more important services."¹⁸

Letters 3 and 4: Bourton to Goodman's Fields
The response from Bourton also consisted of two letters, one from the pastor and the other from the church. In his letter, Beddome expressed his condolences to the Goodman's Fields church as they faced the death of their pastor.¹⁹ He acknowledged the decision to be no small matter for either party.²⁰ He elaborated on the motivations to relocate to London: the Goodman's Fields church was more significant and had more resources; there was also prospect for greater usefulness in the city.²¹ Beddome then listed several reasons for remaining in Bourton: he had been ordained to the church

---

rians. Goodman's Fields Church to Bourton Church, November 11, 1750, in Brooks, *POTP*, 33. It is worth noting that Wilson and Beddome were both referred to as "learned" in this letter. Goodman's Fields Church to Bourton Church, November 11, 1750, in Brooks, *POTP*, 33–34. Beddome had first studied at the Bristol Academy, but then moved to study at an Independent Academy in London under John Eames (1686–1744). Brooks, *POTP*, 22–23.

In 1796, Andrew Fuller (1754–1815) noted that the greater part of the Baptist ministers in the Northamptonshire Association did not have an "academical education." Andrew Fuller, "Discipline of the English and Scottish Baptist Churches," in *The Complete Works of the Rev. Andrew Fuller with a Memoir of His Life by Andrew Gunton Fuller*, ed. Joseph Belcher (1845; repr., Harrisonburg, VA: Sprinkle, 1988), 3:481. Nearly a half century earlier, when the Goodman's Fields church was looking for a learned minister, an even smaller percentage of ministers would have been educated.

17 Dawkes had been called there in 1735 and pastored the church for about sixteen years. After his departure, the church declined through death and removals and eventually dissolved in 1761. For these and other details concerning Dawkes, see Ivimey, *History of the English Baptists*, 3:504–6.

18 Goodman's Fields Church to Bourton Church, November 11, 1750, in Brooks, *POTP*, 34. This final phrase is connected to the concept of usefulness introduced in the previous letter.

19 Benjamin Beddome to Goodman's Fields Church, n.d., in Brooks, *POTP*, 34–36. Beddome called Wilson "an instructor," which could be trace back to the days when Beddome was baptized and called to the ministry while under Wilson's care. Brooks, *POTP*, 23; Ivimey, *History of the English Baptists*, 3:553.

20 For the London church, it concerned their spiritual vitality, and for Beddome, he desired to have a clean conscience over the matter.

21 Beddome's listed the advantages of relocating to London: the church in Bourton was lowly and had much debt, whereas the London church was thriving and affluent. In the country, Beddome seldom enjoyed hearing and fellowshipping with other pastors, but London had "the best of preachers" and brother pastors who were united by a common cause and affection. Beddome was baptized and called to the ministry at Goodman's Fields, and the church sent Beddome to Bourton in the first place; thus, Beddome had a special regard for the London church. Bourton was clearly a place of less influence than London, and he acknowledged the Goodman's Fields perspective that Beddome would be of greater usefulness in the city. Gary Brady says that the Little Prescott Street church was "London's largest Baptist church at the time." Gary Brady, "Being Benjamin Beddome: A Biographical Study," in *Glory to the Three Eternal: Tercentennial Essays on the Life and Writings of Benjamin Beddome (1718–1795)*, ed. Michael A. G. Haykin, Roy M. Paul, and Jeongmo Yoo, Monographs in Baptist History 13 (Eugene, OR: Pickwick, 2019), 13.

there, and strong bonds of affection exited between him and the people.[22] Thus, a divided Beddome said, "I am in a great strait. I cry to God for direction, but what way I shall take, I know not," and entrusted himself to the church who would make the final decision concerning his removal to London or not.[23] Beddome placed the Little Prescott Street church's arguments before his members and instructed them to take a month to pray and talk about the matter before sending a response to London.

The response from the Bourton church was dated December 16, 1750.[24] They expressed sympathy for their friends in Goodman's Fields and agreed "more learned and popular ministers" should be in London since country churches benefited from those in the city.[25] The Bourton church hoped God would raise up a pastor to replace Wilson, though not through "such extremes as to deprive another church of its pastor" as proposed by Goodman's Fields.[26]

The Bourton deacons gave several reasons why Beddome should not relocate to London. The strongest reason was their love and esteem for their pastor. This would have been sufficient to deny London's request, however, the deacons listed several more

---

22 The reasons given for his remaining in Bourton were as follows: first, he was ordained over a people who had treated him with great affection, and many had been converted under his ministry. Second, the church was formerly divided but was now united. Third, Beddome had been fruitful in Bourton, as evidenced by the over one hundred people who were added to the church since his arrival. Fourth, the church's heart was engaged with its pastor. Fifth, they were committed to making Beddome comfortable. And sixth, Beddome had recently recovered from a life-threatening disease, and he attributed his recovery to the care and prayers of his people.

23 Beddome to Goodman's Fields Church, n.d., in Brooks, *POTP*, 36. Benjamin Francis (1734–1799) found himself in a similar situation twenty-two years later when he was requested to remove from his church in Horsley, Gloucestershire, and remove to the Carter Lane church in Southwark, London, to be John Gill's (1697–1771) successor. In a letter to Caleb Evans (1737–1791), Francis expressed the perplexity he felt over the decision—whether to remove or to remain—in a manner akin to Beddome:

> My dear friend, I cannot express the astonishment, the shame, the concern, & perplexity, my mind has been overwhelmed with ever since. The thought of parting with my dear people, & of the unhappy consequences that may follow, dissolves my heart, & almost overpowers my spirits; while on the other hand a pleasing prospect of more extensive & general usefulness presents itself . . . I do not expect to be more happy in a people than I am at present: they love me exceedingly, as I also do them; nor have I but one material thing to complain of here, namely my being obliged to be so much from home, without which I cannot support my family . . . my poor wife is very lonesome & uncomfortable; I shall not be able so well to manage my children ; I cannot visit my people so much as I would; & I have but little time for reading, study, etc. . . . *I am in a great strait*, & my mind is in a state of perpetual suspense. (Benjamin Francis to Caleb Evans, February 22, 1772, in Geoffrey F. Nuttall, "Letters by Benjamin Francis," *Trafodion* [1983]: 7–8 [ellipses original, emphasis added])

For further information and sources on this episode in Francis's life, see Thomas Flint, "A Brief Narrative of the Life and Death of the Rev. Benjamin Francis, A. M.," in *The Presence of Christ the Source of Eternal Bliss. A Funeral Discourse . . . Occasioned by the Death of the Rev. Benjamin Francis, A. M.*, by John Ryland (Bristol, 1800), 42–43, 42*; Michael A. G. Haykin, ed., "Benjamin Francis (1734–1799)," in *The British Particular Baptists, 1638–1910*, vol. 2 (Springfield, MO: Particular Baptist Press, 2000), 17–18; Nuttall, "Letters by Benjamin Francis," 7–8.

24 Bourton Church to Goodman's Fields Church, December 16, 1750, in Brooks, *POTP*, 37–39.

25 Bourton Church to Goodman's Fields Church, December 16, 1750, in Brooks, *POTP*, 37.

26 Bourton Church to Goodman's Fields Church, December 16, 1750, in Brooks, *POTP*, 37.

reasons to buttress their position. They saw their pastor as an answer to prayer—first in his initial arrival in Bourton and second in his recent recovery from sickness[27]—and spoke of his usefulness in the conversion of sinners, increase of membership, and raising of pastors.[28] In light of these reasons, the Bourton church denied London's request for Beddome's removal.

In having read the four letters, one would except the correspondence to have stopped. The city church put forth a strong case for Beddome's removal, but the country church denied the request with equal force.[29] However, like the importunate widow in the Gospel of Luke (Luke 18:1–18), the London church was persistent.[30] After a month and a half, the Goodman's Fields deacons appealed for Beddome to come and pastor the Little Prescott Street church.

Letter 5: Goodman's Fields to Bourton
This second appeal was sent on February 3, 1751.[31] The deacons invoked a "maxim" which they judged to be applicable to all areas of life, whether civil or religious. The maxim was: "The service of all is to be preferred to that of the part. No man ever said that the interest of one member is of equal importance with that of society in general."[32] This premise served as the basis for their appeal in the letter. According to Goodman's Fields, the question was whether the prosperity of Baptist churches in general or the Bourton church alone was to be preferred.

The London deacons claimed Beddome would be more useful by removing to the city than remaining in his "retired station" in the rural region of the Cotswolds. Their ambition for Beddome was he become a celebrated preacher in the city and lend credibility to the Baptist cause, which was often criticized by dissenters and those of the Church of England.[33]

The deacons brought up again the necessity of "an able and learned ministry" being preserved in their midst. In their thinking, only Beddome was a suitable replacement for Wilson. Bourton's insistence on retaining their pastor was based on a concern for Bourton and the surrounding areas only, and not the Baptist cause more broadly. The

---

27 The sickness took place shortly after his marriage to Elizabeth Boswell. Beddome contracted a serious disease that lasted for six weeks and brought him close to the grave. The Bourton pastor recovered, and the whole ordeal endeared the church to their pastor since he saw his restoration as an answer to his people's earnest prayers. Similarly, the fact they nearly lost their pastor strengthened the affection of the people for Beddome. For the information in this paragraph, I am indebted to Rippon, "Rev. Benjamin Beddome," 319.

28 According to Rippon, the men raised up for ministry during Beddome's pastorate were John Collett Ryland, Richard Haynes, John Reynolds Jr., Nathaniel Rawlins, and Alexander Payne. Rippon, "Rev. Benjamin Beddome," 323, 323*.

29 Holmes, "The Early Years," 55.

30 Dix, "'Thy Will Be Done': A Study in the Life of Benjamin Beddome."

31 Goodman's Fields Church to Bourton Church, February 3, 1751, in Brooks, *POTP*, 39–42.

32 Goodman's Fields Church to Bourton Church, February 3, 1751, in Brooks, *POTP*, 39.

33 The argument of the Goodman's Fields church was that Beddome would have been more useful in London and had a more influential and fruitful ministry there. Considering their comments, though, causes one to wonder whether a desire for prestige and respectability had tinged the motives of the London church.

Little Prescott Street deacons could argue this way, of course, because they were in London, and city churches had a more significant impact upon the general interest of the Baptist churches than country churches. Additionally, the impact of city churches on the general cause was proportionate to the quality of its ministers. Consequently, the need of London should have been preferred to that of Bourton. The Little Prescott Street deacons posed a hypothetical scenario. Even if the situation was between the Bourton church and a single church in London—without any consideration of the general interest—Beddome would have been more useful in London than in the obscure village of Bourton.[34] Even in the proposed hypothetical scenario, London was to be preferred.[35]

They gave additional arguments for the propriety of Beddome's removal. The deacons stated the potential of dispersion was greater in London than in Bourton, since their people had forty congregations to which they could disperse. Bourton's fears of dispersion or dissolution, however, were unfounded because they had a suitable replacement in John Reynolds Jr. Additionally, a learned and popular ministry belonged, not in the obscure village of Bourton-on-the-Water, but in the city.

In their letter, Bourton had cited their love and esteem for their pastor as sufficient grounds to refuse London's request. This objection was quickly dismissed by Goodman's Fields since the Bourton church was not considering the general interest and, by their refusal, constraining Beddome's usefulness in the city.[36] The London deacons acknowledged Beddome had been an answer to the prayers of the Bourton church, but they insisted a man with his gifting and graces was "qualified for extensive service" and thus "was not one of those mercies that you can keep or we can take."[37] In a corrective manner, the Little Prescott Street church stated if Beddome discerned he should relocate to London, then Bourton's reluctance could not stop him from accepting the call.[38] The letter concluded with general pleasantries and a plea for a favourable response to their request.

---

34 In the recommendatory preface to Beddome's hymns, Hall acknowledged the obscurity of Bourton, which accorded with the perspective of the Goodman's Fields church. However, with the advantage of hindsight (he wrote nearly seventy years after the correspondence and over twenty years after Beddome's death), Hall also saw the suitability of a gifted and learned man such as Beddome to have spent his days in a country village in the Cotswolds. Hall, "Recommendatory Preface," vi.

35 We have the total membership of the Bourton and Goodman's Fields churches from around that time. Brooks said that the Bourton membership was 180 in 1751, and Ivimey estimated that the Goodman's Fields church had 150 members in 1753. Brooks, *POTP*, 50; Ivimey, *History of the English Baptists*, 3:278. The Bourton church had a larger membership than the Goodman's Fields church. Considering this, the argument made by London here—that even if the situation involved the Bourton church and a single church in London, without regard for the general interest—holds less weight.

36 The London deacons admitted the success of their plan was probable and not certain. To make their case that Beddome would most probably be useful in London, they pointed to Beddome's past successes in Bourton. This was a shrewd tactic, since the Bourton deacons had enumerated these very points concerning Beddome's usefulness in Bourton as reasons for his remaining there.

37 Goodman's Fields Church to Bourton Church, February 3, 1751, in Brooks, *POTP*, 41.

38 Perhaps there was speculation on the part of the Goodman's Fields church that the Bourton church was seeking to retain Beddome even though he was inclined to relocate to London.

Letter 6: Bourton to Goodman's Fields
There were two letters sent in response from Bourton to Goodman's Fields, both signed February 24, 1751. The first was sent by the deacons of the church.[39] While Bourton sympathized with their brethren at Little Prescott Street, they were bothered by the forwardness of the London church.[40] The Bourton deacons asked a hypothetical question to make their point. If a church larger than Little Prescott Street had lost its pastor through death, and they had requested for Wilson's removal—while he was still alive, of course—how kindly would they have looked upon such a request?

The Bourton deacons then responded specifically to the "maxim" put forward by Goodman's Fields. Their response to the maxim was significant since usefulness had been an argument employed by Goodman's Fields from the beginning. According to the Bourton deacons, that a popular and learned minister needed to relocate to the city was not a foregone conclusion. To the contrary, it could be argued eminent ministers were more needed in the country than in the city. Drawing on the imagery in the book of Revelation, the deacons referred to pastors as stars in Jesus's right hand, and thus it was from him that ministers received their brightness and splendor (cf. Rev 1:16, 20; 2:1; 3:1). If Jesus had placed stars to shine in darker parts of the world, their light was more necessary in those places than in other regions where he had set up a constellation of ministers.

The Bourton deacons addressed the claim that Beddome's removal would likely lead to further usefulness in the city. In many cases, when a minister had been removed from a station where God had placed him, it was not accompanied by great success. If ministers had been appointed to a place by God and then were made to leave that station, it could not be assumed they would enjoy continued usefulness. From the vantage point of Bourton, "Usefulness consists not barely in preaching to a very great auditory, but in honouring religion by serving God and our generation in that post in which he sets us."[41]

The Bourton deacons desired to be directed by divine providence. With respect to Beddome's removal, however, they did not see God was leading them this way, since he had been an answer to their prayers. The Bourton church was thankful for city churches helping country churches, but also exposed the problem of country churches always needing to give up their best ministers to city churches.[42] As for Goodman's Fields

---

39 Bourton Church to Goodman's Fields Church, February 24, 1751, in Brooks, *POTP*, 42–44.

40 They wrote, "We are sorry you should desire, much more endeavor, to deprive another church of its fixed pastor, in order to repair the distressing loss of your worthy minister deceased." Bourton Church to Goodman's Fields Church, February 24, 1751, in Brooks, *POTP*, 42.

41 Bourton Church to Goodman's Fields Church, February 24, 1751, in Brooks, *POTP*, 43. The Bourton church admitted the London churches consistently helped country churches. However, if the city churches constantly drew away ministers from the country churches, they were simultaneously helping and harming the churches in the rural areas. Such action on the part of the city churches would lead to friction and division between them and the country churches, since the latter would be deprived of their ministers "whom God has fixed over them, and whom they dearly loved." Bourton Church to Goodman's Fields Church, February 24, 1751, in Brooks, *POTP*, 44.

42 The Bourton church admitted the London churches consistently helped country churches. However, if the city churches constantly drew away ministers from the country churches, they were simultaneously helping and harming the churches in the rural areas. Such action on the part of the city churches would lead

claim that there was no suitable replacement, Bourton retorted they had plenty of good candidates to choose from. In the end, the Bourton church resolutely refused London's request for Beddome's removal. They concluded with a prayer that "the Shepherd of Israel would settle a pastor over you to your joy and satisfaction."[43]

Letter 7: Beddome to Goodman's Fields
In his letter to Goodman's Fields, Beddome reassured the London church he had not influenced his church's decision. On the contrary, he spoke on behalf of Goodman's Fields and strongly put forward their arguments. Even then, however, the Bourton church refused to release their pastor, and so Beddome submitted to the church's will. He provided several reasons for his decision. First, he felt it was not lawful for a pastor to leave his people "without their consent," unless there was serious deficiency on their part, such as lack of love for the pastor, stinginess in giving, divisions, and opposition.[44]

Second, Beddome leaned on the witness of church history. He specifically cited John Owen (1616–1683).[45] Owen believed every local church should seek to promote the welfare of the universal church and thus removals were sometimes appropriate. In these scenarios, a multiplicity of factors needed to be considered. For Owen, the prospect for greater usefulness occasioned the discussion of a pastor's removal from one station to another, but it was not automatic grounds for removal. If a pastor were to relocate to another church, it required the consent of the churches involved and the affirming counsel of other churches and elders of the same denomination.

With respect to Owen's "counsel," the Bourton church had not given their consent to

to friction and division between them and the country churches, since the latter would be deprived of their ministers "whom God has fixed over them, and whom they dearly loved." Bourton Church to Goodman's Fields Church, February 24, 1751, in Brooks, *POTP*, 44.

43 Bourton Church to Goodman's Fields Church, February 24, 1751, in Brooks, *POTP*, 44.

44 Beddome to Goodman's Fields Church, February 24, 1751, in Brooks, *POTP*, 45. Beddome was outlining the basic duties of a congregation towards one another and their pastor. These duties were captured in the sermons to the church at ordination services of English Particular Baptist pastors in the eighteenth century. Beddome had just written that he would not remove to London. Thus, when he claimed that a church's failure in these duties legitimized a pastor's removal, the Bourton pastor was indirectly stating that his congregation had been adequately fulfilling their duties towards him and one another. This whole episode, in fact, had led the church towards deeper unity and paying off a large, long-standing debt.

45 John Owen, *The True Nature of a Gospel Church and Its Government* (London: William Marshall, 1689), 113; see also, p. 112. Owen was leaning on the rulings of the ancient church: once ordained in one place, a bishop or presbyter could not move to another church. This decree was apparently necessary because church officers were making it a habit to move from places of lesser to greater prominence for personal gain. This practice was denounced at the Council of Nicaea in 325 and the Council of Chalcedon in 451. These councils, which are often associated with the respective creedal statements on Trinitarian theology and Christology, issued canons, or laws, that governed ecclesial practice. Owen referred to Canons 15 and 16 from Nicaea and Canons 5 and 20 from Chalcedon. Henry R. Percival, ed., "Excursus on the Translation of Bishops," in *A Select Library of the Nicene and Post-Nicene Fathers of the Christian Church*, ed. Philip Schaff and Henry Wace, Series 2, vol. 14, *The Seven Ecumenical Councils of the Undivided Church* (New York: Charles Scribner's Sons, 1900), 32, 35. For the canons from Chalcedon, see Henry R. Percival, ed., "The XXX Canons of the Holy and Fourth Synods, of Chalcedon," in Schaff and Wace, *A Select Library of the Nicene and Post-Nicene Fathers*, 14:271, 282. It should not be missed that in responding to a contemporary ministerial crisis, Beddome leaned on the wisdom of Owen from the seventeenth century who, in turn, was leaning on the rulings of Nicaea and Chalcedon from the fourth and fifth centuries.

Beddome's removal. Beddome also reported in his letter—and this was the third reason Beddome chose to remain in Bourton—he had consulted friends, fellow pastors, and others who gave the near unanimous advice to remain in Bourton unless the church gave their consent for his removal. The fourth reason was the rarity of success to follow the removal of a pastor. They Matthew Henry (1662–1714) as an example who had left Chester for Hackney in London in 1712.[46]

Beddome then sought to point out a hole in the argument of the London church. If their premise was true—that greater usefulness was sufficient reason for the removal of a pastor—then it would be impossible for smaller and less significant churches to retain their pastors.[47] For Beddome, who ministered in the obscure village of Bourton-on-the-Water, usefulness in another station was one factor to be considered at the prospect of removal and not the deciding element in every case.

John Gill (1697–1771), pastor of the Carter Lane Church in Southwark, London, preached the funeral sermon for Wilson.[48] Beddome said Gill had "entirely left out the prospect of greater usefulness, among the motives which he looks upon as sufficient to authorize the removal of a pastor from one place to another."[49] Of the reasons listed by Gill for the lawful removal of a pastor, the last was a lack of affection between the pastor and the people since that would undermine the effectiveness of the ministry of the Word and ordinances. According to Gill, when there was a strong bond of love between a pastor and his people, it caused the preaching and the administration of the

---

[46] Rather than resulting in greater usefulness, Henry was not overly successful at Hackney, though he labored diligently to the end of his life. As for Chester, Beddome had heard reports that the communicants under Henry were greater than the hearers under his successor, a Mr. Gardiner. For Henry's move from Chester to Hackney, see Allan Harman, "Matthew Henry's Move to Hackney in 1712," *Reformed Theological Review* 80, no. 2 (August 2021): 155–73.

[47] This would also have justified the removal of a pastor in every situation since greater usefulness was nearly always cited as a cause for removal.

[48] Gill, "Reverend Mr Samuel Wilson," in *Sermons and Tracts*, 1:477–98. Beddome evidently had access to this sermon as he referred to it in his letter. For biographical sketches of Gill, see Robert W. Oliver, "John Gill (1697–1771): His Life and Ministry," in *The Life and Thought of John Gill (1697–1771): A Tercentennial Appreciation*, ed. Michael A. G. Haykin, Studies in the History of Christian Thought (Leiden: E. J. Brill, 1997), 7–50; John Rippon, *A Brief Memoir of the Life and Writings of the Late Rev. John Gill, D.D.* (1838; repr., Harrisonburg, VA: Gano Books, 1992). The works of Gill alluded to are John Gill, *A Complete Body of Doctrinal and Practical Divinity: Or A System of Evangelical Truths, Deduced from the Sacred Scriptures* (1839; repr., Paris, AK: Baptist Standard Bearer, 1989); Gill, *An Exposition of the Old and New Testaments*, 9 vols. (1809–1810; repr., Paris, AR: The Baptist Standard Bearer, 2006).

[49] Beddome to Goodman's Fields Church, February 24, 1751, in Brooks, *POTP*, 46. Earlier, Beddome articulated a pastor should not leave his people without their consent except in situations where there was a lack on the church's end. Gill expounded and elaborated on the same concept in his funeral sermon and provided a more expansive list of what could have constituted a lack on the part of the congregation. According to Gill, a pastor may lawfully remove from one church to another if heresies in the church could not be rooted out, immorality was prevalent, discipline was neglected, people refused to submit to Christ's laws, the church could not and would not adequately provide for the pastor and thereby invited the reproach of the world, or "disaffection between him and the people rises so high, on one account or another, that peace and fellowship cannot be maintained, nor the ends of the ministration of the word, and administration of ordinances be answered." Gill, "Reverend Mr Samuel Wilson," in *Sermons and Tracts*, 1:484. There was, as Beddome pointed out, no mention of the prospect of greater usefulness being grounds for the removal of a pastor.

ordinances to be more effective. Therefore, if there was a strong bond between a pastor and people, it was an argument for him to remain in his current station. This thinking accorded with the argument of Bourton and Beddome in their letters.

At this point, Beddome's decision was made: he needed to remain in Bourton. Had he removed to London, it would have been miserable both for the London church and its new pastor, since Beddome would have been acting contrary to conscience. He hoped he had conducted himself uprightly and clarified if his congregation consented to his removal, he would have accepted London's call. Such a departure, though, would have required sacrifice on his part since he deeply loved his people. Since the church refused his removal, however, Beddome concluded, "The will of the Lord be done" (cf. Acts 21:14).[50] The beloved pastor of the Bourton church was resolved that he would not violently tear himself away from his people. Instead, he would rather serve God in a lower and less significant station where God had placed him than "intrude" in a higher and more significant station where God had not directed him.[51]

He concluded the letter by remarking how the whole ordeal—though it came to nothing as far as London was concerned—had caused the Bourton church towards unity and encouraged them to pay off a large and longstanding debt of nearly one hundred pounds.[52] The Bourton pastor urged his friends at Goodman's Fields to wait upon God and, in due time, he would provide for the Little Prescott Street church in ways far better than they could have designed for themselves.[53] He exhorted his

---

50 Beddome to Goodman's Fields Church, February 24, 1751, in Brooks, *POTP*, 46.

51 Beddome to Goodman's Fields Church, February 24, 1751, in Brooks, *POTP*, 46–47. The way the Bourton church sought to discern God's guidance over the matter was different from the approach of Goodman's Fields. Beddome began by asking, "To what station has God called me?" Having determined that (through several factors, not excluding the question of usefulness), the Bourton pastor resolved to be faithful in that place. Goodman's Fields, however, began by asking, "Where will this man be most useful?" with useful being defined as ministering in the most prominent churches and having the largest influence on the greatest number of people from that station. Thus, usefulness, understood in this way, was the supreme consideration above all others. Beddome should have removed to London, according to Goodman's Fields, because he would have been most useful there as a pastor. For Goodman's Fields, the other factors that Bourton cited to argue for the retention of their pastor—the love of the church for their pastor, the reading of Providence that Beddome was God's gift to the Bourton church, the necessity of country churches to have continuing pastors, the danger that Beddome's removal would pose to the country church, and the unanimous decision of the Bourton church to refuse London's request—were all subordinate to the sole consideration of usefulness. To Beddome, this seemed too simplistic an approach.

52 The debt had been incurred through three building projects—the construction of the parsonage in 1741, the expansion of the chapel in 1748, and the strengthening of it in 1750. London's request for the removal of Pastor Beddome and the ensuing deliberations in the church stirred them to pay off these debts. Brooks, *POTP*, 47–48.

53 Even if the worst should happen—which was unlikely—and the Goodman's Fields church were to disperse and significantly decline in numbers, God was able to raise them up as he had done previously. When Wilson came to the church about 25 or 26 years prior, the church was "in a low and declining state," according to Ivimey. Ivimey, *History of the English Baptists*, 3:307. During Wilson's pastorate, the church revived with many people having been converted edified. In his funeral sermon for Wilson, Gill reflected, "The low estate in which you were, when he came to this place, and the numbers of which you now consist, and the flourishing condition in which you now are, abundantly show the success of his ministration among you." Gill, "Reverend Mr Samuel Wilson," in *Sermons and Tracts*, 1:496. In their heartache at the loss of their pastor and the anxiety over his replacement, the Goodman's Fields Church had forgotten their own history.

brethren in London with the words of Psalm 37:5, "Commit, then, your way unto the Lord; trust also in him, and he will bring it to pass."[54] He signed the letter, "Your affectionate and brother in gospel bonds, B. Beddome."[55] Beddome belonged to God as his servant and, in his mind, he was gifted and called by Christ to serve in whatever station his master had placed him. How relieved must the Bourton membership must have been when their pastor read this letter of refusal to London's request at the church meeting on the Lord's Day, February 24, 1751.[56]

Retrieving Wisdom

"Retrieval" is a helpful term to describe the practice of learning from the past. A single lesson will be drawn from this correspondence between the Baptist churches of Bourton-on-the-Water and Goodman's Fields for contemporary Christians and pastors. The lesson was captured by Beddome's biographers, so even in the process of retrieval, I am leaning on earlier writers.

The correspondence demonstrates the propriety of a gifted and learned pastor remaining in the station to which God has called him, even if there is opportunity to remove to a more significant place. That a man of Beddome's caliber ministered for over five decades in the obscure village of Bourton-on-the-Water was not lost on his early biographers. Beddome's memorialist said, "the retirement of Bourton would furnish but few incidents for history."[57] There is irony, of course, in the writing of this article which seeks to retrieve wisdom from letters that were penned in the remote, obscure, village of Bourton-on-the-Water. Later in the memoir, the memorialist spoke of Beddome's usefulness in Bourton, pointing to the increase in membership from roughly 70 to 180, from the time he arrived there in 1740 to 1751, and that 6 men had been called to the ministry during Beddome's pastorate.[58] In a sketch written seventy years after Beddome's death, G. Hester wrote that in Bourton, "he lived a retired, studious, pious, and useful life."[59] Hester's terse statement rebutted any notion that a Christian minister could only be useful in the most prominent and influential places.

Robert Hall Jr. (1764–1831) who captured the peculiar-yet-beautiful picture of an educated and gifted minister who spent his life ministering in a rural village in the Cotswolds of England:

> Though he spent the principal part of a long life in a village retirement, he was eminent for his colloquial powers, in which he displayed the urbanity of the gentleman, and the erudition of the scholar, combined with amore copious vein of attic salt than any person it has been my lot to know. As a preacher, he was universally admired for the piety and unction of his sentiments, the felicity of

54 Beddome to Goodman's Fields Church, February 24, 1751, in Brooks, *POTP*, 47.

55 Beddome to Goodman's Fields Church, February 24, 1751, in Brooks, *POTP*, 47.

56 Brooks wrote, "At the same time the pastor read his answer to the said letter, for which being also in the negative, the church expressed their thankfulness." Brooks, *POTP*, 42.

57 Anonymous, "Memoir," xxi.

58 Anonymous, "Memoir," xxvi.

59 G. Hester, "Baptist Worthies—Benjamin Beddome," *The Baptist Magazine* 57 (January 1865): 443.

his arrangement, and the purity, force, and simplicity of his language; all which were recommended by a delivery perfectly natural and graceful.[60]

These early biographers spoke with one voice that there were lessons to be learnt from this letter exchange between Bourton and Goodman's Fields. The letters penned by the Bourton church and Beddome provided a visible pastoral theology, that is, *pastoralia* in action. Beddome's example provided future pastors with counsel if they found themselves circumstances akin to Beddome's, namely, needing to consider a pastoral move. More broadly, Beddome's decision to remain in Bourton demonstrated to posterity the beauty and legitimacy of a pastor remaining in a station to which God had called him, even if it was a less glamorous and influential place. In other words, bigger was not always better.[61]

---

60 Hall, "Recommendatory Preface," vi.

61 The thinking that bigger is better in pastoral ministry is well-captured by Zach Eswine's testimony regarding his approach to ministry when he was twenty-six and finishing seminary: "It was becoming quite clear to me that if I was to prove successful in ministry, I needed to do something great, and I needed to define something great in terms of how large, famous, and fast I could accomplish it." Zach Eswine, *The Imperfect Pastor: Discovering Joy in Our Limitations through a Daily Apprenticeship with Jesus* (Wheaton IL: Crossway, 2015), 21. The twentieth-century apologist Francis Schaeffer spoke of the temptation facing those engaged in ministry: "All of us—pastors, teachers, professional religious workers and nonprofessionals included—are tempted to say, 'I will take the larger place because it will give me more influence for Jesus Christ.'" Schaeffer continued, "But according to the Scripture this is backwards: we should consciously take the lowest place unless the Lord Himself extrudes us into a greater one.... This is the way of the Christian: he should choose the lesser place until God extrudes him into a position of more responsibility and authority." Francis A. Francis A. Schaeffer, *No Little People* (1974; repr., Wheaton, IL: Crossway, 2021), 34–35. For the quotation from Schaeffer, I am indebted to Eswine, *Imperfect Pastor*, 146.

A review article of David Mark Rathel, *Andrew Fuller and the Search for a Faith Worthy of All Acceptation* (2024)

Pieter Rouwendal

Dr. Pieter Rouwendal is Associate Professor of Historical Theology and Lecturer in Methodology at the Theological **University** *of Apeldoorn, The Netherlands.*

Introduction

Andrew Fuller (1754–1815), though an autodidact, has had a profound influence. Among Particular Baptists of his day, Fuller's theological ideas as written in the *Gospel Worthy of All Acceptation* provided the impetus for William Carey's (1761–1834) missionary work. Nevertheless, his influence transcended his denomination, time, and country, and even the commonwealth. For instance, in 1805, within twenty years of its publication, the Presbyterian church in America resolved that the missionary committee would procure 250 copies of Fuller's *Gospel Worthy of All Acceptation*.[1] The same work was translated into, at least, Dutch (1863 and 2004; new edition in preparation), Spanish (2019), and Portuguese (2020). The translations indicate that there is a growing international interest in the theology of Andrew Fuller.

Fuller broke away from hyper-Calvinism and became its most vigorous opponent. He abandoned the prevailing hyper-Calvinist view of his time and region, which believed that unregenerated people are not obliged to have a saving faith in Jesus, and he returned to a classical Reformed position as expressed for instance in the Canons of Dordt (1618–1619). In contrast, the opinion often labeled as "hyper Calvinism" has not received similar attention. Despite being unpopular, it is necessary to comprehend the opposing perspective in order to gain a comprehensive understanding of Fuller and his response.

David Mark Rathel, Associate Professor of Christian Theology at Gateway Seminary in Mill Valley, California, set out to explain Fuller's doctrine of salvation within its historical context. The result is a book that devotes relatively little attention to Fuller,

---

1 Samuel J. Baird, *A Collection of the Acts, Deliverances and Testimonies of the Supreme Indicatory of the Presbyterian Church, from its Origin in America to the Present Time* (Philadelphia: Presbyterian Board of Publication, [1855], 414–5). The critical edition of this work will be published soon, see Robert William Oliver and Michael A.G. Haykin, eds., *Apologetic Works 1: The Gospel Worthy of All Acceptation*, The Complete Works of Andrew Fuller 5 (Berlin: de Gruyter, 2026).

and a great deal of attention to the views of certain hyper-Calvinists. Rathel turns successively to Joseph Hussey (1660–1726), the "father" of hyper-Calvinism, John Gill (1697–1771), the most learned hyper-Calvinist, and to the "Modern Question" debate about whether unconverted people can be called to saving faith, before finally turning to Andrew Fuller's response. Before delving into these chapters in greater detail, it is first necessary to offer an impression of the whole book.

Rathel's work is of significant value, making a notable contribution to the field of Fuller research. His book represents a significant contribution to the existing literature, addressing a previously unaddressed gap in knowledge. To illustrate, he presents a comprehensive analysis of Hussey's perspectives for the first time, and similarly, he offers a detailed account of the 'modern question' debate for the first time. In several instances, Rathel has corrected previous research on this topic. For instance, he demonstrates that supralapsarianism was not a defining characteristic of hyper-Calvinism, as had been previously asserted. Additionally, he illustrates, based on the context of John Gill's statements, that this theologian did indeed reject the notion of a universal imperative to possess saving faith in Christ. Consequently, his book is an invaluable resource for anyone seeking to comprehend Fuller's *Gospel Worthy of All Acceptation* and related books.

It is regrettable that a book of such importance is marred by significant shortcomings. From a methodological standpoint, the book suffers from the issue of some quotations and references being challenging to verify, while some others are found to be inaccurate or unreliable upon verification. In terms of content, a significant issue arises when Rathel contextualizes Fuller within the framework of hyper-Calvinism without adequately situating this concept within its historical and theological context. He presents a series of factors that led hyper-Calvinists to adopt their position. However, the history of the emergence of this idea is more complex. Indeed, a conclusion that Calvinists may find challenging to accept is that it is much more deeply rooted in mainstream Calvinism than is often thought. To these factors that have been overlooked in the emergence of hyper-Calvinism, I will first turn my attention. I will then highlight some theologians who were important for Fuller but have been ignored. Finally, I will review the first three chapters of the book.

Ignored factors
Rathel is inclined to identify single and straightforward causes. In the initial phase of hyper-Calvinism, the doctrine of "eternal salvation" served as the rationale for the repudiation of the obligation to adhere to the tenets of faith. In a subsequent phase, the focus shifted to Adam's inability to embrace saving faith in Christ. However, the rejection of the obligation to have faith is the result of a multitude of factors, which were perceived by its proponents as consistent with Reformed theology, even as an inevitable consequence. The various elements that may have collectively or independently contributed to the denial of the duty of unregenerate individuals to believe in Christ should not be overlooked. Consequently, an examination of the factors that appear most significant to me will be presented. Further investigation into these factors is necessary.

A first factor was the doctrine of predestination. Since the time of Augustine

(354–430), this doctrine has been charged with the objection that it made exhortations superfluous. Calvin and other Reformed theologians had to answer this objection in their own time.[2] The Reformed consistently refuted this objection; nevertheless, the issue of divine predestination and human responsibility was intrinsic to Reformed theology. The hyper-Calvinists appeared to validate their opponents' assertions and eschewed exhortations to saving acts like faith. Fuller recognized the necessity to confront the hyper-Calvinistic argument from election, as he recognized it in the second objection to his doctrine in part three of his *Gospel Worthy of All Acceptation*. Another factor was the doctrine of limited atonement. When Christ has not died for all, but only for the elect, then the question must be faced of how everyone, even those for whom Jesus did not die, can be called to believe in him with the promise of being saved. The mainstream Reformed tradition upheld a general invitation to Christ with this promise, but this approach faced inherent challenges within Reformed theology.[3] The question of particular redemption, which the hyper-Calvinists sought to address in a different manner than the mainstream Reformed, was a long-standing point of contention within Reformed history. Fuller addressed this issue as the third objection to his doctrine in part three of his *Gospel Worthy of All Acceptation*.

A third factor was the question of the nature of faith, its location in the understanding or in the will, and the way those who do not yet believe may be exhorted. During the Reformation period, the prevailing view was that faith constituted a knowledge of God's benevolence towards the individual. Assurance was an intrinsic aspect of faith. However, considering the doctrine of predestination and particular atonement, it is pertinent to question whether it is genuinely feasible to exhort all individuals to embrace a personal faith in God's benevolence towards them through Christ. This question was introduced into the Reformed agenda through the debate with the Lutherans. The debate was further intensified by Jacobus Arminius' (1560–1609) reasoning, which posited that the necessity of belief in the atonement of Christ for the salvation of humanity necessarily entailed the actuality of Christ's death for all. This conclusion was not one that the Reformed theologians were willing to accept. In response, some proposed an alternative interpretation, suggesting that faith does not immediately lead to this knowledge but rather develops through stages. Consequently, they argued, everyone is not immediately obliged to believe that Christ died for them, but rather indirectly, after other acts of faith or convictions have taken place. The result is that one must have a warrant of faith, which is to say, one must conclude that one has already attained a previous stage of faith. This consequence was absolutized by some hyper-Calvinists, but it was already stated by mainstream theologians such as Heinrich Alting (1583–1644). Others, such as William Ames (1576–1633) and Samuel Rutherford (1600–1661), posited that the act of faith is not contingent on the knowledge that sins have been forgiven, i.e. in the mind (or, intellectualism), but in the outgoing act of the soul towards Christ as Savior who can also save me, i.e. in the will (or, voluntarism). The conviction that Christ has died for a person does not form

---

2 See Pieter L. Rouwendal, *Predestination and Preaching in Genevan Theology from Calvin to Pictet* (Kampen, the Netherlands: Summum, 2017).

3 For instance, see the Canons of Dordt 2:5.

part of the act of faith itself but rather emerges as a consequence of it.[4] Theologians such as Hussey and John Brine (1703–1765) can be situated within the tradition of thinkers like Alting, who espoused an intellectualist perspective. Fuller, on the other hand, embraced a voluntaristic approach to faith, addressing the question of what faith is at the outset of his *Gospel Worthy of All Acceptation*. The first part is completely devoted to it.

A fourth factor was the dispute between the Reformed and the Remonstrants concerning the efficacy of moral suasion. The Remonstrants held the view that a resistible moral suasion was sufficient for the purpose of conversion, whereas the Reformed emphasized the necessity for an irresistible work of the Spirit. Hyper-Calvinists presented a contradiction to these two positions, in a manner similar to the Remonstrants. In contrast, the mainstream Reformed theologians maintained that, although moral suasion is inherently ineffective for salvation, the Spirit employs it to convert sinners to God through his quickening power. This dispute constituted a fertile ground for the growth and flourishing of hyper-Calvinism. Fuller addressed this as the fifth objection in part three of his *Gospel Worthy of All Acceptation*.

Finally, the hyper-Calvinists hammered on a general Protestant conviction, namely that grace is given and not earned by or dependent on any act of man. That receiving grace is not ultimately dependent on faith either, while faith is a condition for salvation, the mainstream Reformed resolved by teaching that justifying faith itself is a gift from God. The hyper-Calvinists went a step further by denying the conditional nature of faith as such.

One might inquire as to why Rathel chose to disregard these factors. He interprets Fuller's *Gospel Worthy of All Acceptation* primarily and almost only as a refutation of the hyper-Calvinistic argument from Adamic inability to believe, but this is not the full picture. Fuller's responses to objections demonstrate the presence of additional arguments beyond the Adamic inability, which Rathel repeatedly highlights. Others, such as John Stevens, opposed Fuller's answers to objections from the doctrines mentioned above.[5] Rathel's contextualization of Fuller is commendable. However, for those seeking to comprehend the theology Fuller rejected, it is essential to consider the five factors that contributed to the emergence of hyper Calvinism.

Ignored theologians
Given the preceding research on hyper-Calvinism, Rathel's focus on Hussey and Gill is understandable. An examination of the "modern question" debate is beneficial for contextualizing Fuller's *Gospel Worthy of All Acceptation*. Nevertheless, there were other theologians who as well had influence on Fuller's ideas in the sense that he distanced himself from them. The ideas of the Sandemanians for instance, who were no hyper Calvinists, but who sprouted from the same trunk—antinomianism. It is a term Rathel rarely uses, preferring to label men like Tobias Crisp (1600–1643) and

---

4 Johan N. Mouthaan, *Belofte en bevel: De universaliteit van de belofte en de plicht tot geloof in de gereformeerde orthodoxie (1620–1650)* (Apeldoorn, the Netherlands: Labarum, 2024).

5 John Stevens, *Help for the True Disciples of Immanuel: Being an Answer to a Book Published by Andrew Fuller, on the Duty of Sinners to Believe in Christ; Which Book Is by Him Mis-Called, the Gospel Worthy of All Acceptation* (London: C. Whittingham, 1803).

John Eaton (1575–1641) as "contra-Puritans." By speaking about the antonominians, William Huntington (1745–1813) should have been mentioned, who was abhorred by Andrew Fuller, yet remained a very popular hyper-Calvinist preacher. Furthermore, Fuller bought the works of Huntington to write his *Picture of an Antinomian*, and Huntington in turn attacked Fuller.[6]

John Skepp (1675–1721)
While Rathel demonstrates an ability to read and interpret with great care, he also exhibits instances of inaccurate reading. For instance, he asserts—or rather reiterates previous research—that John Skepp was a disciple of Hussey and a link between Hussey's and Gill's theological perspectives. Skepp's *Divine Energy* "focused on a single issue—the use of 'moral suasion' in gospel preaching. He attacked the use of 'reasonings and arguments' in gospel presentations and derided gospel offers as 'criminal.'"[7] However, Skepp did not deride a gospel offer in his book, nor did he attack moral suasion or the use of reasonings and arguments. The word "criminal" is used by Skepp for preachers who think moral suasion is enough without the work of the Spirit, and manage it "in a direct opposition to, and with reproaching of God's sovereign efficacious grace, and the invincible efficacy of his Spirit and power."[8] This is not exactly the same as what Rathel makes of it. It is even exactly the opposite of what Skepp remarks in the very context of the quotation above:

> That God doth, for the most part, make use of arguments and reasonings in the Word and ministry; and oft points and enforces the same, with promises of rewards, and threatnings of present and future punishments to the neglecters of so great salvation; yet so, as that he always superadds the efficacious power of his Spirit and Grace, to quicken and renew those souls, for whom he has had an eternal purpose of love and grace; by which power he effectually works in them both to will and do. And hence it is, that in the Gospel parts of the Old and New Testament so frequently meet with exhortations, invitations, expostulations, and arguments used with the chiefest of sinners; and these back'd with suitable promises and incouragements: and also, on the other hand, there is an use made of counsel, admonition, and threatnings; yea, and of the sharpest reproofs, to such as are obstinate and rebellious. … These, then, are a sort of adjuncts, or necessary concomitants attending the ministry of the word; as it relates to some part of man's duty, who is always to be treated with as a reasonable creature, and not as a brute beast, or senseless machine. And therefore this way of reasoning, either with saints or sinners, is not to be discarded out of the ministry, nor

---

6 Andrew Fuller, *The Complete Works of the Rev. Andrew Fuller*, 3rd ed. (Harrisonburg, VA: Sprinkle, 1988), 1:74. For instance, see G.M. Ella, ed., *Weighed in the Balance. Exccommunicating the Sheep in Order to Feed the Goats* (Millbank, London: Huntingtonian Press, 1998).

7 David Mark Rathel, *Andrew Fuller and the Search for a Faith Worthy of All Acceptation: Exploring Fuller's Soteriology in Its Historical Context* (London: Bloomsbury, 2024), 57.

8 John Skepp, *Divine Energy: Or the Efficacious Operations of the Spirit of God Upon the Soul of Man in His Effectual Calling and Conversion, Stated, Prov'd and Vindicated. Wherein the Real Weakness and Insufficiency of Moral Suasion (without the Superadition of the Exceeding Greatness of God's Power,) for Faith, and Conversion Tot God, Are Fully Evinced. Being an Antidote Against the Pelagian Plague* (London: Joseph Marshall, 1722), 41.

slighted or turned to another meaning.⁹

Furthermore, this quote calls into question whether Skepp was a hyper-Calvinist in the first place! The quoted sentences give the impression that Skepp was rather mainstream Reformed concerning moral suasion and the work of the Holy Spirit.

In addition, Rathel cites the first edition of 1722 in his bibliography, but obviously quotes from the third revised edition of 1815.[10] Rathel's method of citation and interpretation is such that it renders his source to say the exact opposite of what it actually says. Furthermore, it makes it challenging to control his quotation by using a different version as referred to. This is a serious detriment to the otherwise worthwhile book. A comparison with Fuller's third proposition in the second part of the *Gospel Worthy* shows a striking similarity with the words of Skepp: "Prop. III. The Gospel, thought it be no law, but a message of pure grace, yet virtually requires such an obedience to it which includes saving faith."[11] Fuller did not refer to Skepp. But he could have done so. Further research into Skepp is necessary to ascertain his proper place in the theological landscape of his era. He was indeed a member of Hussey's congregation for a period before he became a Baptist, and he was highly valued by John Gill. However, the aforementioned quotation makes clear that this does not necessarily make him a hyper-Calvinist.

Thomas Goodwin (1600–1680)

A theologian who is not ignored, but whose great influence is not fully acknowledged, is Thomas Goodwin. Through Goodwin, some peculiarities entered English theology. One is a supralapsarian Christology, which Goodwin borrowed from the medieval theologian Duns Scotus (c.1265/6–1308). It entails situating the decree of the incarnation of God the Son above the decree of the admission of the fall, as well as the decree of union with God of the elect.[12] Rathel is excused for failing to discern this, for even Mark Jones failed to notice it in his dissertation on Goodwin's Christology.[13] Yet it is Goodwin's supralapsarian Christology that permeates Hussey and Gill. Goodwin's contributions also included a Scotistic structure of predestination. The election to glorification occurred supralapsarian, with the passing or rejection of others, yet without a decision concerning the ultimate destination of those others. In consequence of the decree of the fall, a second form of election of the elect in Christ took place, namely, to be saved also by Christ. The decision of damnation of the rejected also takes

---

9 Skepp, *Divine Energy*, 42.

10 The word "criminal" in relation to moral suasion is not on page 41 in the 1722 edition, but on page 59 of the 1815 edition. Rathel refers to page 59.

11 Andrew Fuller, *The Gospel of Christ Worthy of All Acceptation: Or the Obligations of Men Fully to Christ, and Cordially to Approve, Whatever God Makes Known. Wherein is Considered the Nature of Faith in Christ, and the Duty of Those Where the Gospel Comes in that Matter* (Northampton, 1785), 57.

12 Thomas Goodwin, "Discourse of Election, of the Free and Special Grace of God Manifested Therein; the Absoluteness and Unchangableness of His Decrees; and Their Infallible Accomplishment," in *Works of Thomas Goodwin D.D.*(London: Darby and Roycroft, 1683), 2:[121]–456.

13 Mark Jones, *Why Heaven Kissed Earth: The Christology of the Puritan Reformed Orthodox Theologian Thomas Goodwin (1600–1680)* (Göttingen: Vandenhoeck & Ruprecht, 2010).

place infralapsarian.¹⁴ This structure is evident in the work of John Gill, who, while not rejecting infralapsarianism, exhibits a distinct inclination towards the structure proposed by Goodwin.¹⁵

A third input from Goodwin is the place he assigns to the Holy Spirit in *pactum salutis*. Rathel recognizes this, but traces Gill's similar position back not to Goodwin, but to Hussey. Indeed, Hussey was likewise influenced by Goodwin, but since Gill does not adopt Hussey's views on the eternal God-man, there is much to be said for Gill's direct reference back to Goodwin and not to Hussey in this instance. The impact of Goodwin--who was never before accused of having contributed to the emergence of hyper-Calvinism--on Hussey and Gill, demonstrates that the emergence of hyper-Calvinism was a gradual process that developed out of mainstream Calvinism, a perspective that Rathel's analysis does not fully acknowledge.

Overestimated Factors
Rathel repeatedly states that the covenant theology of Crisp, Hussey, and Gill played a pivotal role in the development of hyper-Calvinism. They designed a covenant theology wherein *foedus gratiae* and *pactum salutis* were identified. Christ took upon himself all the conditions of the covenant for the elect, leaving no condition at all for them to fulfill. It appears that this covenant theology was indeed coherent with hyper-Calvinism. However, I question Rathel's assertion that it was the primary cause. The Scottish theologian Thomas Boston (1676–1732), for instance, also espoused a similar covenant doctrine.¹⁶ Despite this, Boston and the other theologians of the "Marrow Controversy" did not disavow the call to faith or the offer of grace; instead, they rejected the idea that the universal offer was conditional. It demonstrates that this form of covenant doctrine does not inevitably lead to hyper-Calvinism.

However, the simultaneous rejection of faith as a condition and the call for personal faith might be perceived as an internally inconsistent stance. Andrew Fuller acknowledged this and concluded that the system espoused by Boston and his colleagues was, in essence, also conditional. In answer to the unconditional scheme of a Mr. Anderson, an American adherent of the Marrow theology, Fuller wrote:

> I have no partiality for calling faith, or any thing done by us, the condition of salvation; and if by the term were meant a deed to be performed of which the promised good is the reward, it would be inadmissible. If I had used the term, it would have been merely to express the necessary connexion of things, or that faith is that without which there is no salvation; and, in this sense, it is no less a condition in Mr. A.'s scheme than in that which he opposes.¹⁷

14 See Goodwin, "Discourse of Election."

15 See John Gill, *A Complete Body of Doctrinal and Practical Divinity; or a System of Evangelical Truths, Deduced from the Sacred Scriptures* (London, 1795), 1:257–280.

16 Thomas Boston, *A View of the Covenant of Grace from the Sacred Records: Wherein the Parties in That Covenant, the Making of It, Its Parts Conditionary and Promissory, and the Administration Thereof, Are Distinctly Considered: Together with the Trial of a Saving Personal Inbeing in It, and the Way of Enstating Sinners Therein unto Their Eternal Salvation. To Which is Subjoyn'd, a Memorial Concerning Personal and Family-Fasting and Humiliation, Presented to Saints and Sinners* (Edinburgh: R. Fleming, 1734).

17 Fuller, *Complete Works*, 2:336–7.

It is worthy to note that both hyper-Calvinism and Marrow theology have their origins in a rejection of neo-nomianism. This has resulted in the pursuit of unconditional grace, predicated on an unconditional covenant for the elect and an unconditional approach to gospel preaching. However, whereas the hyper-Calvinist preached an unconditional gift to the elect alone, the Marrow-men contended for an unconditional offer to all. When viewed solely in terms of their respective modes of preaching, these two positions appear to be diametrically opposed. Nevertheless, when the underlying theological principles are considered, the similarities are striking. It demonstrates that the covenant view was not a defining aspect of hyper-Calvinism.

The concept of the "eternal pactum salutis" is a key element of Rathel's understanding of "eternal salvation." In other words, Rathel maintains that salvation was established in eternity rather than in time. This is a complex and contentious issue. First, it is notable that Hussey and Gill employed the term "eternal salvation," but in a manner that signifies a salvation that will never end. Andrew Fuller utilized these words in this sense. Rathel appears to utilize the term in a manner that differs from that of Fuller. He appears to suggest that salvation was not merely decreed in a pre-temporal eternity but rather established in that realm. This presents a challenging topic: the relationship between time and eternity. There are, at the very least, two ways in which this relation can be described. One perspective is to conceptualize time and eternity as a unified continuum, devoid of origin and without an endpoint. Within this framework, time is understood as the delineated and constrained portion of this continuum where creation exists. This model divides eternity into three parts: a pretemporal eternity, time as part of eternity, and post-temporal eternity (Model A). An alternative representation of this relationship is to conceptualize time and eternity as two distinct categories. In this perspective, eternity is not an infinite temporal sequence but an absence of time, a state of "eternal present." Time is not a component of the unending continuum of eternity but a wholly distinct category (Model B). In this model, eternity precedes time in a structural sense but not in a chronological one.

Model A: linear

pretemporal eternity	time	post-temporal eternity
	creation last day	

Model B: separate

◯
eternity   _____
                     time

A third model should be considered, in which model B is applicable to God, but parts of model A are relevant to human beings, who begin to live in time but enter a post-temporal eternity upon death. For them, there is no pretemporal eternity, and post-temporal eternity might signify for them an endless succession of time (Model C: integrated). The relationship between temporal human beings and eternity demonstrates the complexity and, ultimately, the inconceivability of this matter. It is a subject that requires further investigation, but my impression is that most Reformed theologians adhere to this integrated Model C.

Model C: distinct for God and human beings
God:

○   ———————

eternity   *time*

Humanity:

time	post-temporal eternity
creation *last day*	

It appears that Rathel espouses the perspective of Model A, as evidenced by his frequent references to "pretemporal eternity." At least, Rathel appears to ascribe this perspective to Hussey and Gill. It is unclear whether Rathel is espousing this viewpoint, as he does not explicitly state it. It is possible that Hussey or Gill or both had this concept regarding time and eternity. Nevertheless, I am skeptical of this assertion. A review of their published works did not yield any evidence of the term "pretemporal salvation," nor even the word "pretemporal." Rathel must demonstrate that Hussey and Gill subscribed to Model A to substantiate his assertions regarding "eternal salvation." However, should evidence emerge indicating that they espoused Models B or C, Rathel's conclusions would inevitably falter. If they espoused model A, then "eternal justification" would signify that the elects were justified from the moment of creation, or from the moment of their conception, as Crisp appears to have asserted. However, given that Hussey and Gill characterized "eternal justification" as an immanent act within God in eternity, it is uncertain whether they intended to convey this interpretation. When they adhered to model B or C, it simply does not follow.

Models B and C require a high level of abstraction. In the context of theological discourse, the decree of God in eternity does not refer to something in the future, but rather to something in time. However, given that God's eternity is an eternal "present" or an eternal "now," there is no chronological distinction between decree and execution, only a distinction in structure. This renders the concept of "eternal justification" more conceivable, and it demonstrates that it does not imply a pre-temporal justification. The differentiation between time and eternity and the way they are and are not related is pivotal for a comprehensive understanding of this concept. Regrettably, Rathel does not address this distinction.

The real problem for Rathel, in making "eternal justification" a mark or at least immediate cause of hyper-Calvinism, is that it would be necessary to classify Fuller as a hyper-Calvinist. Rathel acknowledges that Fuller espoused the doctrine of eternal justification for approximately a decade following his refutation of hyper-Calvinism.[18] This discrepancy renders his emphasis on the pivotal role of eternal justification in hyper Calvinism perplexing.

---

18 Rathel, *Andrew Fuller and the Search for a Faith Worthy of All Acceptation*, 140–142.

Joseph Hussey

Rathel's chapter on Joseph Hussey is most welcome. It is the first investigation to this remarkable theologian since Peter Toon's (1939–2009) publications in the 1960's. While Toon primarily leaned on Hussey's *God's Operations of Grace but No Offers of Grace* (1707), Rathel shows Hussey had already moved towards hyper-Calvinistic ideas in his *Glory of Christ Unveiled* (1706). Unfortunately, Rathel cites from an unpublished edition of Hussey's *Glory of Christ Unveiled* by Mark Jacobson, not the original work. It makes it hard to check him. Rathel tries to do justice to Hussey by exploring his motives for arriving at hyper-Calvinistic ideas and by being objective. According to him, Hussey's theology grew out of the antinomianism, or what he calls the "contra-Puritanism" of Tobias Crisp and John Eaton. These preachers maximized God's grace and justification without works. They sought to remove all conditions from the proclamation of the gospel, rejecting the use of the law to bring sinners to Christ and the use of external evidence or marks to determine one's spiritual condition.[19]

Hussey added his concept of the God-man Jesus Christ. He borrows heavily from Goodwin but makes some important modifications. Hussey seems to suggest that Christ's human nature already existed in eternity in the negotiations of *pactum salutis*, which Goodwin did not say. Rathel looks for sources of Christ's pre-existence. Rathel argues for Isaac Watts' (1674–1748) influence on Hussey, not because Hussey quotes Watts, but vice versa.[20] However, Watts began publishing a volume of verses in the same year Hussey published his *Glory of Christ* and works in which Watts wrote about the pre-existence of Christ's soul were published later.

Regarding the conversion of sinners, Rathel states that Hussey affirmed "that in Adam even the elect received a 'corrupt nature near of kin to the devil.'"[21] The reference is to the unpublished and edited edition mentioned above, so it is difficult to verify. The words marked as quotations are not found in a digital search of the original text. The last six words are found six times in Hussey's *Glory of Christ*, but he always denies that the elects are "near of kin to the devil."[22] Again, Rathel's method of quotation is inaccurate. Nevertheless, his conclusion that according to Hussey, the mystical union with Christ did not end with Adam's fall is correct. Hussey stated this even more passionately. Nevertheless, it is incorrect to state that Hussey understands conversion as nothing more than receiving knowledge of eternal justification. For Hussey, a "motion-faith," on the refuge-cities is understood as "So here again, 'tis set out by flying for refuge, without staying to consult whether these poor creatures were not too filthy to go to Christ by faith? No, they run in and never laid any such obstacle in their own, or other Men's way. These believers in the sight of a necessary, present cleansing themselves, did hasten in without dispute, without delay."[23] The experienced need to be cleansed and the sinner's flight to Christ are incompatible with the Holy Spirit merely informing

---

19 Rathel, *Andrew Fuller and the Search for a Faith Worthy of All Acceptation*, 8–9, 21.

20 Rathel, *Andrew Fuller and the Search for a Faith Worthy of All Acceptation*, 35.

21 Rathel, *Andrew Fuller and the Search for a Faith Worthy of All Acceptation*, 42.

22 Joseph Hussey, *The Glory of Christ Unveil'd: Or the Excellency of Christ Vindicated in His Person, Love, Righteousness* (London, 1706), 552, 578, 583–5, 588.

23 Hussey, *Glory of Christ*, 482.

him of his eternal justification. For Hussey, in God's eternity, the elects never fell from grace and from Christ. But in human time, he seems to have regarded them as born unclean and far from Christ. Rathel's statement that according to Hussey the fall "only introduced 'obstacles' and 'impediments' in their relationship with [God]," is again unverifiable.[24] In the original the words marked as quotes are not digitally found in the same way.

Rathel's chapter on Joseph Hussey is most welcome in that it offers more information than Peter Toon's publications. But it is not accurate in all respects. More research on Hussey and his sources is needed to understand his influence on and role in the emergence of hyper-Calvinism. The most pressing question that this chapter—and the chapter on Fuller—leaves unanswered is the relevance of Hussey to Fuller. Rathel almost denies its relevance, for Hussey did not object to obligatory faith from Adamic inability, and this was Fuller's primary target. Fuller used Hussey to object to his opponents that Hussey did not hold this position. But Rathel does not acknowledge all the places where Fuller refers to Hussey. And these references by Fuller are important.

The first concerns Hussey's exegesis of John 5.40, as Fuller wrote:

> Mr. Hussey understands the foregoing passage of barely owning Christ to be the Messiah, which, he says, would have saved them as a nation from temporal ruin and death; or, as he in another place expresses it, "from having their brains dashed out by the battering rams of Titus," the Roman general. But it ought to be observed that the life for which they were "not willing" to come to him was the same as that which they thought they had in the Scriptures; and this was "eternal" life.[25]

Fuller rejected Hussey's idea of the kind of faith to which unbelievers might be urged, but this aspect is neglected by Rathel. Rathel also fails to examine Fuller's misquotation of Hussey in his reply to William Button (1754–1821), where Fuller insists that according to Hussey unregenerate people have a duty to listen spiritually and open their hearts to Christ. This is precisely what Hussey denied.[26]

John Gill
John Gill is far better known than Joseph Hussey, who was one of the most influential Baptist theologians. Most of my criticisms of this chapter regarding *pactum salutis* and "eternal salvation" is mentioned above.

For Rathel, Gill "presented faith as a mere passive acknowledgement of God's prior work."[27] However, it seems that such a view is contrary to Gill's chapter on faith in *Body of Divinity*, where he described faith as related to the *person* of Christ rather than to his work. Gill elaborated on faith in the elements of knowing Christ, assenting to Christ, loving Christ, and depending on Christ, and as mentioned by the names of (the acts of) seeing Christ, coming or fleeing to Christ, a venturing act of their souls on Jesus,

---

24 Rathel, *Andrew Fuller and the Search for a Faith Worthy of All Acceptation*, 42.

25 Fuller, *Complete Works*, 2:356.

26 Fuller, *Complete Works*, 2:423.

27 Rathel, *Andrew Fuller and the Search for a Faith Worthy of All Acceptation*, 67.

a casting themselves in the arms of Christ, laying hold on Christ, retaining Christ, leaning on Christ, but "[t]he grand and principal act of faith … is receiving Christ."[28] These acts are much more than just a passive knowledge. There is some truth in Rathel's statement, but presenting only this element without mentioning the acts of faith is making a caricature of Gill's ideas.

Rathel's idea that Gill's distinction of God's acts in internal and external acts perhaps originated from Hussey is absurd.[29] Furthermore, Rathel argues that Gill was an infralapsarian, as Gill places justification from eternity under the fall.[30] Since justification refers to men as sinners, it is necessarily infralapsarian. Nevertheless, while Gill did not reject infralapsarianism, he preferred supralapsarianism.[31] Rathel is confused by Gill's distinction—in turn borrowed from Thomas Goodwin—between a supralapsarian election of persons and an infralapsarian decree concerning the means of salvation. He makes a similar mistake concerning John Brine, as Rathel claims that Brine used Gill's writings to describe how infralapsarianism cohered with eternal justification.[32] Brine used Gill's distinction between a decree concerning persons and concerning the means of salvation, but election as such is still supralapsarian. He explicitly stated, "an act of preterition was pass'd on the apostate Spirits, considered as unfallen."[33]

As with Hussey, the big question that Rathel leaves partially unanswered is the relationship between Gill and Fuller. Fuller frequently refers to Gill as an authority and for an exegesis that Fuller rejects. Rathel explains the positive references to Gill as strategic, but it seems more likely that Fuller genuinely appreciated Gill. In fact, Fuller accepted Gill's doctrine of eternal justification until many years after the publication of The Gospel Worthy. This was not a strategy; it was conviction. Rathel acknowledges that Fuller found in Gill's theology the distinction between the "power of the hand" and the "power of the heart." Such a distinction was fundamental to Fuller's theological development as he applied it to the lack of power of faith. Fuller's relationship with Gill was one of both appreciation and distance. It was more complex than the flat relationship that Rathel paints.

The Modern Question Debate
Rathel's chapter on this debate is perhaps the most important, since the "Modern Question" debate is the immediate context of Fuller's *Gospel Worthy of All Acceptation*, and it is the first investigation of several works written in this debate. The debate is named after a pamphlet by Matthias Maurice (1684–1738), *A Modern Question Modestly Answer'd* (1737). The question was "Whether the Eternal God does by his Word make it the Duty of poor unconverted Sinners, who hear the Gospel preach'd

---

28 Gill, *Complete Body of Doctrinal and Practical Divinity*, 3:59–60.

29 Rathel, *Andrew Fuller and the Search for a Faith Worthy of All Acceptation*, 62.

30 Rathel, *Andrew Fuller and the Search for a Faith Worthy of All Acceptation*, 78.

31 See Gill, *Body of Doctrinal and Practical Divinity*, book 2, chapter 2.

32 Rathel, *Andrew Fuller and the Search for a Faith Worthy of All Acceptation*, 100.

33 John Brine, *Remarks Upon a Pamphlet, Intitled, Some Doctrines in the Superlapsarian Scheme Impartially Examin'd by the Word of God* (London, 1736), 8.

or publish'd, to believe in Jesus Christ?"[34] On the front page of his pamphlet, Maurice quoted Isa 8:20 as an indication that he would answer the question only from the Bible, as Maurice eschewed any systematic theological argument. He compiled thirty texts which he felt made it clear that unconverted sinners have the duty to believe in Christ.

Rathel points out that Maurice came from hyper-Calvinistic circles and he admired Hussey and Richard Davis (1658–1714). It seems to be strange that while acknowledging Maurice's appreciation of Hussey and Davis, Rathel does not acknowledge Fuller's sincere appreciation for John Gill. Moreover, it is still an open question why Gill did not actively engage in the Modern Question debate. It seems that Gill had already offered the main arguments used by hyper-Calvinists to refute Maurice in his the *Cause of God and Truth* (1735), in which, Gill frequently stated that the faith to which people are called in preaching is a historical faith, not a saving faith.[35] Rathel's single focus on Adamic inability to believe, while ignoring other factors in the Modern Question debate, is already rebutted by the pamphlet that ignited the debate, as Maurice addressed several objections to the idea that all people have the duty to believe in Christ. These include election and particular redemption.[36] It further disproves Rathel's idea that Lewis Wayman (d. 1764) accepted the conditions set by Maurice—viz. arguing only from scripture—and avoided the subject of salvation in eternity.[37] However, Wayman's third chapter is entirely Husseyan in arguing from the different relationships Christ has with the church and with the rest of creation, and the relation with the church was made before the foundation of the world.[38]

Regarding the nature of faith, Rathel sticks to what is called a natural faith and to which all people may also be called according to hyper-Calvinists.[39] But he does not analyze what was the nature of saving faith according to the hyper-Calvinists or their opponents. One of the fundamental questions here is: Is saving faith the conviction that one is a child of God, or that Christ died for one and that one is saved (as some hyper-Calvinists held) or is it an acceptance of Christ as the only one who can save me (as most of their opponents held)?

Conclusion
Rathel took a good subject to write a book about. He studied several publications for the first time, or for the first time in years, which makes his book worthwhile. Notwithstanding all my criticisms, this praise should be given. Any researcher of

---

34 Matthias Maurice, *A Modern Question Modestly Answer'd* (London, 1737), 3.

35 For instance, see his exegesis in this book on John 1:7, "the external revelation ... only requires an historical faith, or bare assent to the truth of the said propositions. Now such faith is not saving" (John Gill, *The Cause of God and Truth: Being an Examination of the Principal Passages of Scripture Made Use of by the Arminians, in Favour of their Scheme; Particularly by Dr. Whitby, in His Discourse on the Five Points: In which the Arguments Sounded on the Said Passages of Scripture, are Answer'd; the Objections Taken from Them Removed, and the Genuine Sense of Them Given* [London, 1735], 1:150).

36 Maurice, *Modern Question*, 22–25.

37 Rathel, *Andrew Fuller and the Search for a Faith Worthy of All Acceptation*, 94.

38 Lewis Wayman, *A Further Inquiry after Truth. Wherein Is Shewn What Faith Is Required of Unregenerate Persons; and What the Faith of God's Elect Is, Which Is a Blessing of the Covenant of Grace* (London, 1738), 44–51.1738

39 Rathel, *Andrew Fuller and the Search for a Faith Worthy of All Acceptation*, 105–7.

Andrew Fuller's theology can benefit from this book. But it is clear that this book will not be the final one and should not be the last one on the conviction that Fuller opposed—hyper-Calvinism; rather, this book shows how much research remains to be done to clarify hyper-Calvinism, its arguments and its developments, and thus, to clarify the context of one of the most influential Baptist theologians—Andrew Fuller.

The Journal of Andrew Fuller Studies
10 | Fall 2025

Texts & documents

A newly discovered letter by Joseph Kinghorn (1766–1832)
Transcribed by Daniel Reed
Annotated and introduced by Baiyu Andrew Song

Daniel Reed PhD is a research associate of Oxford Brooks University, and a Farmington Institute research fellow. He was public engagement manager for the Oxford Centre for Methodism and Church History until 2024.

Baiyu Andrew Song PhD, FRAS, is a senior fellow of Andrew Fuller Centre for Baptist Studies. He serves as adjunct professor at Redeemer University, Ancaster, Ontario and Carey Theological College, Vancouver, BC.

Introduction

Dr. Daniel Reed and I met at last year's conference at Exeter, where I presented a paper on the Baptist communion controversy in the eighteenth century.[1] Shortly after my session, we were scheduled to visit the library at Exeter Cathedral. While waiting outside of the cathedral, where the statue of Richard Hooker (1554–1600) stands, Daniel and I chatted about Joseph Kinghorn (1766–1832), who I only briefly mentioned in my paper. While telling me that he grew up in Bishop Burton, in the east riding of Yorkshire, where Kinghorn also grew up, Daniel told me that he purchased a letter written by Kinghorn a few years ago. I was astonished, as I had come across an original letter on sale before, but it was too late for me to purchase it. I am thrilled that Dr. Daniel Reed has transcribed the whole letter and has allowed me to annotate and publish it in the *Journal of Andrew Fuller Studies*. Besides the manuscript, I am delighted that a unique friendship was formed over a shared interest in Joseph Kinghorn.[2]

With the rise of the Royal Mail, letter-writing became a unique genre and

---

1 The conference "Writing Faith and Place in Early Modern Britain" (April 17–19, 2024) was organised by David Parry, Philip Schwyzer, and Niall Allsopp, at the University of Exeter.

2 On Joseph Kinghorn, see Martin Hood Wilkin, *Joseph Kinghorn, of Norwich* (Norwich: Fletcher and Alexander; London: Arthur Hall, 1855); C.B. Jewson, *The Baptists in Norfolk* (London: Carey Kingsgate, 1957); Baiyu Andrew Song, "'The Steady Obedience of His Church': The Ecclesial Spirituality of Joseph Kinghorn and the Communion Controversy, 1814–1827" (PhD diss., The Southern Baptist Theological Seminary, 2023).

phenomenon in the long eighteenth century.³ Particularly, for those who were separated, letters dissolved their physical distances and created a form of conversation where the senders and the recipients could exchange news and ideas. Joseph Kinghorn and his parents David (1737–1822) and Elizabeth Kinghorn (1738–1810) kept up a correspondence from the former's first apprentice at Hull in 1779 till the latter's removal to Norwich in 1800. Since paper was still comparatively expensive, Kinghorn filled the space with lengthy theological discussions.⁴ Besides their theological values, these letters also document the development of the parents-son relationship while providing insights into socio-political changes in Bishop Burton and Norwich. After Joseph Kinghorn's death, Simon Wilkin (1790–1862) and Martin Hood Wilkin (1832–1904) took the former's belongings into their custody.⁵ Besides compiling a catalogue of Kinghorn's library, Wilkin also arranged and numbered his letters, which was done to write a biography of the Norwich minister.⁶ It seems that while the majority of Kinghorn's letters were stored in the vestry of St. Mary's Baptist Chapel in Norwich, some were either sold or given to Baptist antiquarians.⁷ It was not until the late twentieth century, through the labour of C.B. Jewson (1909–1981), a large number of family papers and correspondence between Joseph Kinghorn and his parents were donated to the Baptist Union Library, which were later transferred to the Angus Library and Archive at Regent's Park College, Oxford.⁸ Further discoveries at the Baptist Historical Society and purchases and donations from various sources made Angus Library and Archive the host of the greatest number of Kinghorn's papers and correspondence.⁹

In addition, Jewson also created the Simon Wilkin Letters collection, which primarily contains letters written to Kinghorn from Wilkin and other Baptist leaders, such as Andrew Fuller (1754–1815), John Ryland, Jr. (1753–1825), and William Steadman (1764–1837).¹⁰ Despite being a smaller collection, the Simon Wilkin Letters

---

3 See Susan E. Whyman, *The Pen and the People: English Letter Writers 1660–1800* (Oxford: Oxford University Press, 2009).

4 On paper trade, see Patricia Hernlund, "William Strahan's Ledgers, II: Charges for Papers, 1738–1785," *Studies in Bibliography* 22 (1969): 179–95; Daniel Bellingradt, "The Paper Trade in Early Modern Europe: An Introduction," in *The Paper Trade in Early Modern Europe: Practices, Materials, Networks*, ed. Daniel Bellingradt and Anna Reynolds (Leiden, the Netherlands: Brill, 2021), 1–30.

5 See "Will of Reverend Joseph Kinghorn, Dissenting Minister of Norwich, Norfolk," October 4, 1832, PROB 11/1806/381 (National Archives, Kew).

6 [Simon Wilkin, ed.,] *Catalogue of the Entire Library of the Late Rev. Joseph Kinghorn, of Norwich* (Norwich: Wilkin and Fletcher, 1833); Wilkin, *Joseph Kinghorn*.

7 For instance, Thomas Philpot (1774–1857), minister of the Baptist congregation in Histon, Cambridgeshire, collected letters to and by Joseph Kinghorn. See Thomas Philpot Collection, D/PHI (Angus Library and Archive, Regent's Park College, Oxford).

8 Kinghorn Papers, D/KIN (Angus Library and Archive, Regent's Park College, Oxford). Jewson also noticed that ten letters, either addressed to or written by Kinghorn, were destroyed during the Norwich Blitz in 1942. For the list, see C.B. Jewson, "Calendar of Letters to and from Joseph Kinghorn," FC 6/27 (Norfolk Record Office, Norwich).

9 According to the catalogue composed in 1999, four items were purchased by the Baptist Union Library in June 1967. Forty-five letters were found among the papers donated by the Baptist Historical Society. One letter was purchased at auction in 1992. Kinghorn's birthday prayers were donated by Kenneth Hipper, the archivist of St. Mary's Baptist Church, in May 1997. Another letter was purchased in 1984.

10 Simon Wilkin Letters, MS 4281 (Norfolk Record Office, Norwich). In my previous works, I wrongfully referred to this collection as Wilkin Papers, which is a different collection. See Wilkin papers, MC

are valuable in two ways. First, the collection reveals the uniqueness of Kinghorn's correspondence with his parents, as he rarely spent the same amount of ink to discuss his theological and spiritual reflections with others. Second, the Simon Wilkin Letters also provide significant contexts for Kinghorn's mature years after 1800, especially since the Norwich minister became more involved on the national stage. Besides Oxford and Norwich, the Baptist Historical Preservation Society, the John Rylands University Library, and the British Library also hold letters by and to Joseph and David Kinghorn.[11] Nevertheless, there are still significant gaps in Kinghorn manuscripts.

The following text, which was discovered and purchased by Dr. Daniel Reed, is significantly rare, as no letter between Kinghorn and his parents written in the year 1788 can be found in any of the above-mentioned archives.[12] Nevertheless, the year 1788 was significant for Joseph Kinghorn. In August 1784, a year after his baptism, Joseph Kinghorn went to Bristol and studied under Caleb Evans (1737–1791). While at the academy, Evans sent Kinghorn and other students to preach at various neighbouring congregations. In 1785, during his first visit to Fairford, Kinghorn told his parents that since the death of Thomas Davis (d. 1784), students from Bristol were requested to supply the pulpit, as a horse was provided and "the student stays two Sabbaths and then returns."[13] Arriving on March 4, 1785, Kinghorn preached twice on Sunday, March 7, and preached in the evening of Wednesday, March 9, and again on Sunday, March 14.[14] The extract in Wilkin's biography does not indicate Kinghorn's first impression of the Fairford congregation. Nevertheless, Kinghorn informed his parents of his discovery

64/12, 508X8 (Norfolk Record Office, Norwich).

11 I am grateful to the late Rev. Terry L. Wolever (1958–2020), who kindly provided scanned copies of these letters. Wolever also owned a letter from James Hinton (1761–1823) to Joseph Kinghorn, which was published as "Appendix C: Letter from James Hinton to Joseph Kinghorn, 1788" in *The British Particular Baptists: Volume V. More Biographical Essays of Notable British Particular Baptists*, ed. Michael A.G. Haykin and Terry Wolever (Springfield, MO: Particular Baptist Press, 2019), 437–40. The letters held in the John Rylands Library are transcribed by Timothy D. Whelan, ed., *Baptist Autographs in the John Rylands University Library of Manchester 1741–1845* (Macon, GA: Mercer University Press, 2009), 147–8, 172, 180. The British Library holds five letters from Joseph Kinghorn to John Rippon (1751–1836), see Letters to John Rippon, collections related to Bunhill Fields, MSS 25386-9, 28513-23, 56412-18 (British Library, London). I am grateful to Dr. Timothy D. Whelan for providing information about the collection.

12 A letter from James Hinton to Joseph Kinghorn (November 27, 1788) is the only one written in 1788. See James Hinton to Joseph Kinghorn, November 27, 1788, D/KIN 2/1788, #479 (Angus Library and Archive, Regent's Park College, Oxford).

13 Wilkin, *Joseph Kinghorn*, 84. This Thomas Davis is to be distinguished from Thomas Davis of Reading (1734–1796); about the latter, see Michael A.G. Haykin, *Holy Spirit Now Descend: Thomas Davis and the Evangelical Revival in Georgian Berkshire* (Brighton: Ettrick, 2022). According to Isaac Taylor (1776–1810) of Calne, Wiltshire, whose father and grandfather were members of the Fairford Baptist congregation, "the reverend, pious, and judicious Mr. Thomas Davis, for forty years pastor of the Baptist church at Fairford, was much spoken ill of by the carnal people of the place, and some of my father's servants were as ready therein as any others. One thing in which that man of God was vilely slandered was respecting what he said at the funeral of a child to its parents; many persons falsely asserting that he addressed them in the following words, 'If you have not done as you ought to have done by this child, the devil will tear you to pieces, as pigs tear colewort leaves.' And having often heard the same repeated by others, I soon had it frequently in my own mouth; and once being out in the fields with some of my father's work people, to divert them at meal-time, I told them I would preach a sermon to them. Accordingly, having turned up a hurdle end-ways against a gate-post, to serve for a pulpit, I got to the top of it, and altering the aforesaid sentence to suit my purpose, made choice of it for my text, and addressed my auditory as follows: 'If you don't do as you ought to do, the devil will tear you to pieces as pigs tear colewort leaves.' And with a considerable harangue on the subject, I greatly diverted the silly company. Pardon my sin, O Lord, for it is great" (J.W., "Isaac Taylor, of Calne, Wilts," *Baptist Magazine* 53 [November 1861]: 694).

14 Wilkin, *Joseph Kinghorn*, 84.

of a massive collection of Jonathan Edwards' (1703–1758) works in Davis' library.[15] As he had only read Edwards' memoir and some sermons before, Kinghorn told his parents that he intended to read "as much as may be," and he expressed his admiration of Edwards, as he stated that "such a life did I never read, [Edwards] seems to live a heaven on earth, and in abilities he was unrivalled, although his learning was not very extensive. But might I be any man I ever heard of or saw it should be Jonathan Edwards."[16]

Though Kinghorn revisited Fairford in May 1786, it was not until September 1787 that the Fairford congregation made an invitation to Kinghorn, asking him to be their probationary pastor.[17] As Kinghorn's study at Bristol drew to an end, he became anxious about where to minister. In early 1787, Kinghorn became a candidate for the Baptist congregation in Oxford. Despite the fact that James Newton (1734–1790) and Robert Hall, Jr. (1764–1831), both tutors at Bristol, "thought none of the students fit for Oxford but [Kinghorn]," the congregation instead chose Kinghorn's friend James Hinton (1761–1823). Kinghorn then went back home to visit his parents in the summer. He returned to Bristol around the same time the Fairford invitation arrived.

In January 1788, Joseph Kinghorn moved to Fairford, where he spent six months on probation. Despite Kinghorn's attachments to friends in the congregation, the relationship between Kinghorn and the congregation began to sour as early as March 1788. In the letter to his parents, dated March 25, 1788, Kinghorn stated that "the congregation is a good deal mixed respecting sentiments; some are for very high rigid Calvinism, such as they will never get from me."[18] As a result, it was rumoured that Kinghorn preached Arminianism. He became "quite popular in the country round for heterodoxy. Suspicious whispers, and I know not what besides, have made those with whom I never was acquainted, think me a dangerous being."[19] As the following text shows, Kinghorn revealed his impression of the Fairford congregation to his father and expressed his desire to resign. Nevertheless, as Kinghorn told his father in a previous letter, he enjoyed fellowship with neighbouring Baptist ministers such as Benjamin Beddome (1717–1795), Daniel Turner (1710–1798), and Benjamin Francis (1734–1799).[20] With other ministers, Kinghorn also helped a small group of Baptists in Arlington.[21]

Text
> Dear Father & Mother
> Fairford August 21..1788
> Yours of the 2^د. [August 2, 1788] I rec^د. in due course I was very glad to find you

---

15 Wilkin, *Joseph Kinghorn*, 84.

16 Wilkin, *Joseph Kinghorn*, 84.

17 Wilkin, *Joseph Kinghorn*, 111.

18 Wilkin, *Joseph Kinghorn*, 117.

19 Wilkin, *Joseph Kinghorn*, 117.

20 Wilkin, *Joseph Kinghorn*, 125.

21 Wilkin, *Joseph Kinghorn*, 125–6.

were so much better than before as I hope you continue so.²² Your Letter gave me great pleasure altogether tho by some of the Questions you ask I confess I am ^put^ a little to a stand Especially by those particular Enquiries concerning my Situation both in general as respects the State of the Church & in particular as relates to the State of my own mind. There are so few pleasing circumstances that attend either the one or the other when I look at them [deletion] at large that perhaps from any view more pain than pleasure will arise.²³ But that I may give you a pretty fair statement in answer to your enquiries––as to the place I like it well enough tis not the most pleasant nor the most unpleasant in this respect I think it equal if not superior to B[ishop] Burton & also healthy. On this account I should be content to stay if other things were suitable & if not I could leave the <u>place</u> without much regret. As to the Inhabitants of F[airford] I am acquainted with very few except our own ^people^ who are not many several of our Congregation coming from the Country. And as to the people who hear me & with whom I am most connected tho I once entertained a high opinion of them yet I find (taken them in the general) ^they^ are people <u>of very little reading or reflection & consequently very little Intelligence is to be</u>

---

22 This letter cannot be located in any known archives.

23 The congregation at Fairford was first organised around 1700, when a licensed house in Meysey Hampton was used for worship. The congregation then erected a chapel in 1723 at Fairford, "but preaching was continued in the same private house until prevented by the intolerant interference of the incumbent of the parish" ("Maiseyhampton," *The New Baptist Miscellany* 6 [Supplement, 1833]: 617). The congregation's first minister was Thomas Davis (d. 1784), a student from Bristol, who arrived in 1744 and ministered till his death. From 1784 to 1793, the congregation was supplied by neighbouring ministers and Bristol students.

Kinghorn first visited Fairford in March 1785 and returned on Christmas day, 1787. The congregation invited Kinghorn in January 1788 to "to spend six months with them on probation, at the conclusion of his studies in the following May" (Wilkin, *Joseph Kinghorn*, 115). Though Kinghorn also received an invitation from Dereham, Norfolk, to succeed Thomas Wright (d. 1787), a Norfolk farmer, who never was ordained but ministered to the new congregation for three years. Later, when Kinghorn moved to Norwich, he developed a close friendship with its minister Samuel Green (1770–1840), who was ordained in 1797. Regarding the Fairford congregation, Kinghorn told his parents: "As to Fairford, I have an invitation from the church, signed by all present but two. I am much more convinced of the attachment of my friends than before, and I was much afraid if I did not go they would leave the church, indeed, I am almost certain the principal men would: this made me take the opportunity to beg of them to consider the welfare and peace of the church as a part of the church of Christ, in which little parties and passions should be entirely laid aside, and that, if I should come, they would still endeavour to promote the interest of the whole; and after I had talked in this way to one I went to another, and told him what I had said, that I might read him the same lesson in an indirect manner. It had the desire effect, so far that they assented to it, and said they wished me to speak my mind quite openly, and they thought it was very good in me to consider them thus" (Wilkin, *Joseph Kinghorn*, 115–116).

As this letter reveals, Kinghorn's experience at Fairford was not pleasant, as he later learned that "the opposition against my coming is stronger than I thought it was" (Wilkin, *Joseph Kinghorn*, 117). Due to different theological positions, many in the congregation became suspicious of Kinghorn and falsely accused him of being "a dangerous thing," preaching heterodoxy (Wilkin, *Joseph Kinghorn*, 117). Despite Caleb Evans' efforts to defend his student, the conflict was not solved. In April 1788, David Kinghorn advised his son to "preach [the rumour down]," by treating "practical subjects doctrinally and on doctrinal subjects practically" (Wilkin, *Joseph Kinghorn*, 121). Kinghorn explained that he "preached those things that most affected my own mind, and I do not think my views of the gospel, as a system of entire mercy, are at all diminished. When I preached in your pulpit, I enjoyed much pleasure myself, and you and your people were pleased to express satisfaction in my attempts to set forth the unsearchable riches of Christ to sinners, in saving them from sin and hell, and making even the poor of this world heirs of an immortal kingdom, in ruling over his enemies and guiding his people through the intricate mazes of human life to his heavenly mansions; and I am not sensible that at F[airford] I preached any other Gospel. I have laboured to convince them that Christ died for sin and rose again for our justification, and if this is not gospel, I must confess myself ignorant of it. I have pressed on them as much as I was able, the great guilt of men in not receiving the gospel on this very consideration, that in rejecting the gospel of Jesus they rejected the only way of salvation, which was through him; and surely this is the doctrine which will exalt Jesus and debase men" (Wilkin, *Joseph Kinghorn*, 120).

Learning of his situation, Caleb Evans advised Kinghorn to leave, as he told Kinghorn: "I miss you greatly, and wish you were nearer to me, but it is God that fixes the bounds of our habitations" (Wilkin, *Joseph Kinghorn*, 130).

expected among them. Indeed sensible people here of any description are very scarce or however I have not sense to find them out. I have a few whose welfare I sincerely desire & who I doubt not bear the same good will in all its extent to me. On the account of these I feel an Inclination to stay as perhaps my stay might in some degree increase their happiness—but there are but a few for whom I am particularly concerned. I also should have no objections to stay if matters prove at all tolerable in order to preserve the Ch^h from ruptures Divisions & Strife which will most certainly (upon all the principles of human foresight) take place.[24] Should I leave them & besides after this attempt they will not find it easy to get a Minister who will trust himself among them from the Academy. They can scarcely have any Hope in the Country they are getting a bad name as an obstinate litigious set of people. Now on these grounds for I wish to go in such a manner as shall be for <u>general good</u> & I think I can say that particular likings or dislikings to places &c does not in the least biass my mind. Some Circumstances which once had some influence my mind do not now operate with the force they once did[25] but this only turns my attention to the general state of things & leads me to ask what ought I do for the best taking in all together. Now whether I have given you satisfaction or not I can scarce tell. These are the views that I have & on which I wish to act I am almost afraid to go away & yet scarce know what to think of staying. If I stay my private enjoyments must be independent of the People in a great measure at least for a considerable Time & indeed my Happiness will be very little connected with them

[p. 2]
tho I may expect pain from them. On the most favourable supposition I cannot expect more than two thirds of the people to be [deletion] ^for my stay^. & I very much fear the others will be thorns in my side & on the whole be enemies. Tis true we are now quiet but tis not a peace which may at all be depended on. I really think an open rupture would on the whole be more safe. They be perpetually at the catch at every thing I drop from the pulpit & in some instances will go quite opposite to their own Sentiments to get a blow at me. Those men who are exactly of my Sentiments will be heard & every thing they say taken in good part every thing that I say that at all approaches particular Sentiments is suspected as being only a veil under which other notions are concealed. These things give me very little concern. Those who act in this way are men whose Minds about any Sentiments are so contracted that they are not worth minding. ex nihilo nihil fit.[26] only such things are disagreeable & not only ^as they^ affect me so much as the state of the Ch^h. For my part I should be very well pleased if the effects of these things extended no farther than to myself for I think Fools amuse no dispraise. But a few ignorant bigoted obstinate people who

---

24 Curiously, the church minute book only began to record a list of members, a covenant, and church meetings in 1793, when Daniel Williams (1759–1841) was called to minister the congregation. Kinghorn's name was not mentioned at all. See "Baptist Church Book, Fairford (1780–1843)," D4278/2/1 (Gloucestershire Archives, Gloucester).

25 JK's note at this point: "you will ask what I mean I reply I had once a higher idea of some of the people here than I now have respecting some the more I know the more I dislike them this makes me [sp...?] and this is all I mean by what I have said above."

26 Loosely translated as "out of nothing, nothing is produced," or "from nothing comes nothing."

always are attended with a number of people whom they turn at their pleasure may do more evil in a Society than all the wise Men can do good. However by this I don't wish to be thought complimenting my own party for there is not one of them joined to the Ch^h.. that I think worthy the appellation of a candid sensible Man or at least with only an exception or two—& what is still worse I look on the greater part of them as incurable. Owing to their Education prejudices & Age many of them are so benumbed that their minds have no spring at all this I apply to many who are for my stay. You recommend insisting on practical religion for some weeks past I have been almost entirely on such subjects & as led to enforce it—perhaps I may have been usefull I know not—but I have many times thought of what was remarked of a reformer that he found old Adam too hard for young Melanchthon.[27] Indeed I find too little of the influence of religion in my own mind to expect I should be able powerfully to impress others. We are Gods husbandry but tis difficult to bring forth fruit worthy the tillage we have received. These things I own taken all together are not very pleasing but I must say the appearance at Arlington very pleasing & was I to stay here I oft think it would be my delight.[28] I am afraid you will be cast down at this relation ^but^ for tho it is disagreeable yet there is no knowing how matters will turn I find my mind waned in many Instances so that it does not so press me down as it did & as I am pretty easy I wish you to be so—tho hope may die yet God lives & tho men are so unstable that I oft think I'll trust them no more yet God is an unchangeable Friend to those that look to him. I am I hope thankfull that my Health is in a much better state than when I last wrote & that it has been for some time since the Fever is abated & my Strength & Spirits returned in a great measure & as the sultry weather is now gone I hope I shall continue better. I am rather at a loss for proper society seldom meeting with any much calculated to raise but rather to depress I confess I don't find my Grey-heads at all but those [deleted] from whom any thing is

---

27 When Philip Melanchthon (1497–1560) experienced conversion, he "thought it impossible for his hearers to withstand the evidence of the truth in the ministry of the gospel; but, after preaching awhile, he complained, 'That old Adam was too hard for young Melancthon [sic]'" (Erasmus Middleton, *Biographia Evangelica: Or, an Historical Account of the Lives and Deaths of the Most Eminent and Evangelical Authors or Preachers, Both British and Foreign, in the Several Denominations of Protestants, from the Beginning of the Reformation, to the Present Time* [London, 1779], 1:490). It is unclear where Kinghorn got this quote, though the phrase "God's husbandry" in the following sentence seems to suggest that Kinghorn was familiar with John Flavel's (c.1627–1691) *Husbandry Spiritualized: Or, the Heavenly Use of Earthly Things*, in *The Whole Works of the Reverend Mr. John Flavel, Late Minister of the Gospel at Dartmouth in Devon* (Paisley, 1770) 6:187. According to Simon Wilkin's (1790–1862) catalogue, Kinghorn owned the complete works of Flavel, which was the cited 1770 edition.

28 Arlington, Gloucestershire is about six miles north of Fairford and seven miles east of Cirencester. It is said that a Baptist chapel was erected in 1747 for probably a General Baptist congregation. This is probably the reason why Arlington is not included in John Rippon's (1751–1836) list. However, the congregation did not seem to have any minister till the nineteenth century. In a letter to his parents, dated July 22, 1788, Kinghorn mentioned that he and a young Independent pastor from Chedworth routinely supplied the pulpit at Arlington every Sunday evening. Kinghorn loved the people at Arlington, who were "most of them poor, but with that plainness and earnestness in their looks which has a very pleasing influence on the mind. I have great hopes, through the blessing of God, some good will be done by us. Something rather promising than already appeared. A few weeks ago a man who had never gone to any place of worship was asked by a party of people coming to meeting, if he would go, he consented, and thought I was aiming at him all the while; however, he has come and attended, apparently with seriousness, ever since" (Wilkin, *Joseph Kinghorn*, 125–126).

[p. 3]
to be learnt at least many of them.[29] I adopted Elihu's maxim "I said days should speak &c till I am quite tired of it.[30] I reverence Age but I see tis not age only that teaches Wisdom I know there is no loss in being not of the way of those given to Levity but in being almost constantly with those who never seem to grasp an idea nor enter into the Spirit of Conversation is very tormenting. I grant tis not always so I sometimes meet with those who can converse agreeably on the lighter parts of Literature & sometimes enjoy conversation that enters into the spirit of religion so that on the whole I perhaps ought not to complain & while Health is spared I can always find entertainment. I am sometimes vexed by at being against my will exposed to Company which tho good in itself yet dull & unimproving & a variety of things has made me sometimes indulge a reverie & think how much more on some accounts I could enjoy it if I was possessor of a Cot in a lonely place out of the World & away from the Storms of human passions if only I could procure Books where in retirement I could read Life away & enjoy with a favorite author a satisfaction unknown to the avaricious & turbulent & then come out on the Sabbath to preach to the People. I wish to have the pleasure of knowing but I'm thankfull I don't at present feel any anxiety about living & dying in Obscurity—as to the World & the inhabitants of it unknowing & unknown I can come at more usefull Books than in many places I should have the opportunity of doing. The Presbyterian Minister here & my very intelligent Neighbour M[r]. Dore are in these things very kind.[31] I have scribbled up

---

29 In a previous letter to his father, dated July 22, 1788, Kinghorn stated that "Our meeting [at Fairford] when I am in the pulpit looks like a company of old veterans commanded by a boy, for I do not know one in the congregation, (children and servants excepted,) who is not older than myself, and I am almost surrounded with grey heads" (as quoted in Wilkin, *Joseph Kinghorn*, 126).

30 Job 32:7ff

31 The Presbyterian minister refers to Josiah Townsend (1752–1819), who was the son of Meredith Townsend (1715–1801), grandson of John Townsend (1685–1766). John Townsend was a Baptist minister, who assisted Edward Wallin (1678–1733) in Southwark. Growing up under his father's ministry, Meredith Townsend experienced conversion after hearing a young man's sermon. He was baptised by Samuel Wilson (1702–1750) of Prescott Street in 1733. After studying the doctrine of baptism, Meredith became a paedobaptist in 1742/3 and was excluded from the Prescott congregation (Samuel Wilson, "The Baptist Board Mission, 1728–1750," *Transactions of the Baptist Historical Society* 5.2 [1917]: 225). Between 1742 and 1746, Meredith Townsend served as an assistant to Isaac Watts (1674–1748) and Samuel Price. In 1746, Meredith went to Hull and ministered with Tobias Wildboar (d. 1759). In April 1752, Meredith moved to Stoke Newington to succeed Samuel Snashall (fl. 1737–1752), where he ministered till 1789. He then moved to Bath, where he died on December 13, 1801 (see John Tickell, *The History of the Town and County of Kingston Upon Hull* [Hull, 1796], 818–819; W.W., "Some Account of the Rev. Meredith Townsend," *Monthly Repository* 14.168 [December 1819]: 717–719).

Josiah Townsend studied at Daventry under Caleb Ashworth (1722–1775). In 1776, he was ordained to minister the congregation at Rotherham, Yorkshire, where he married Sarah Moult (d. 1812), daughter of Samuel Moult (1718–1776), Townsend's predecessor (for the Moult-Townsend family tree, see John W. Clay, ed., *Familiae Minorum Gentium: Diligentiâ Josephi Hunter, Sheffieldiensis, S.A.S.* [London, 1894], 1:18). In 1787, Townsend moved to Fairford, where he ministered a small Presbyterian congregation till 1796, when he moved to Elland, near Halifax, Yorkshire. He then moved to Mansfield, Nottinghamshire. Theologically, Josiah Townsend was a Socinian (J.W., "Obituary," *Monthly Repository* 14.165 [September 1819]: 512–513).

William Dore (d. 1791) was born to an Anglican family in Hampshire (see S. Reader to William Lepard Smith, July 6, 1778, in "The Late Rev. James Dore of Maze Pond," *Baptist Magazine* 39 [April 1847]: 209–210). Not much is known about his early life, but it is known that he was the eldest son with three younger brothers: David, Thomas, and James (1764–1825)—David and Thomas were baptised and joined the Lymington congregation in 1777. According to the minute book of Lymington Baptist Church, William was baptised by Isaac Stradling, shortly after the latter's ordination, on June 21, 1772, and he was received into full communion on August 2, 1772. A year later, on July 4, 1773, the minute book records that "Brother Dore was calld to the work of the ministry, having exercised his Talents several times among us. The 30th of the same Month,

almost all my paper—as I'm much better I shall not think now of coming home tho a few weeks ago before your Letter arrived I seriously thought of it. I wish I could prevent you from being uneasy at the account I have given. the above Circumstances may pain you as being new & perhaps unexpected but remember they are old to me ^and have lost their edge^ I confess they sink me when I come to sit down & think over all Circumstance but I drive them out of my mind as much as I can. Next week God willing I go to Bristol & hope to take matters over with my Old Tutor & Friend M^r. Evans of whose Kindness I hope I shall ever be mindfull.[32] I have at Times much Fatigue but I know not how I gain nothing by indolence out of Weakness I am strong & I think I may say Strength is equal to my day. As to your remarks on what I wrote I did not design to draw you in to answer mine. Tho I'm pleased you have done it for I really think that where an Objection proves too much it proves nothing. Now it appeared to me that the difficulty you mentioned would as I have said make equally against all the other things I mentioned & if it could not be admitted as of any form against the one neither c^d. it avail against the other. My paper will not admit it or else I think I could prove I am right & make use of your remarks to stabilise my argument which it [unrecognisable] are not far off. Your illustration of the divine agency by Medicine I think very happy consistent with Scripture & the moral powers of Man. I wish I could fill another Sheet or take a shorter essay by conversation to convey my Sentiments on a variety of things. Baxters Saints rest

---

being recommend^ed^ by this Church he went to the Academy at Bristol" (Lymington Baptist Church, Church Book, 1693–1854, 84056/1 [Hampshire Archives, Winchester], [10–11]). According to Cirencester Baptist Church's minute book, Dore arrived in August 1775 to supply pulpit. The congregation did not have a pastor since 1761, and it significantly declined to having only seven members (Joseph Ivimey, *A History of the English Baptists* [London: Isaac Taylor Hinton; Holdsworth & Ball, 1830], 4:480). In response to the Cirencester congregation's call, Dore was dismissed from Lymington on July 21, 1776, and he was ordained on August 20, 1776. Under Dore's ministry, the congregation grew in numbers, and the meeting house was enlarged in 1778. The congregation received financial support from the trust of Abraham Atkins (c.1716–1792) from 1783, and due to Atkins' requirements, the congregation at Cirencester practised open communion (see Ernest A. Payne, "Abraham Atkins and General Communion," *Baptist Quarterly* 26.7 [1976]: 314–319). Dore died on July 3, 1791, and was buried in the chapel under the pulpit ("The Rev. Mr. William Dore," in John Rippon, *The Baptist Annual Register, for 1790, 1791, 1792, and Part of 1793* [London, 1793], 269).

In his letter, dated July 22, 1788, Kinghorn told his father about his neighbouring Baptist congregations and their ministers, including Benjamin Beddome and William Wilkins (c.1752–1812) at Bourton-on-the-Water, Gloucestershire; Thomas Dunscombe (1748–1811) at Coate, Oxfordshire; Daniel Turner (1710–1798) and John Evans (1755–1814) at Abingdon, Berkshire; William Dore at Cirencester; a Mr. Smith at Wantage, Berkshire; Benjamin Francis (1734–1799) at Horsley, Gloucestershire; Joseph Burchell (1743–1826) at Tetbury, Gloucestershire (Wilkin, *Joseph Kinghorn*, 125).

32 Joseph Kinghorn studied under Caleb Evans from 1784 to 1788. For Evans, Kinghorn was "a pupil I could wish him to be, attentive, diligent, respectful, modest, ardent" (Wilkin, *Joseph Kinghorn*, 99). In one of his letters, Kinghorn told his parents that soon after his arrival, Evans asked him: "if I was called out to preach? I replied I could not say precisely; I thought so, but I would tell him how the affair had been proceeded in, and then he could judge whether it was what was so understood; and then giving him a relation of the various circumstances at Newcastle, &c., he said he looked on me as called out to preach; and said he did not suppose I should receive any other call, to which I replied, I thought it not very likely" (Wilkin, *Joseph Kinghorn*, 77). Though Evans did not allow first-year students to preach, he made an exception for Kinghorn, as in October 1784, Kinghorn told his parents: "The Lord's day after Mr. Evans thought I looked pale, and said he thought a ride would do me good; he sent me out to Kingstanley, in Gloucestershire, (I went on the Saturday and came home on the Monday) there I preached twice to a few rough country people; in the forenoon from Psa. cxix, 25, and in the afternoon Eccles. xii, 13. I was a good deal hampered, yet not flustered, in the morning, and being determined to make no haste, spoke in a much more deliberate manner than I used to do. In the afternoon I enjoyed a good deal of serenity of mind and calmness, with such a view of my subject as enabled me to speak with pleasure" (Wilkin, *Joseph Kinghorn*, 74). Since 1787, Evans tried to find a congregation for Kinghorn to minister, among those were congregations in Oxford, Fairford, Chester, Dereham, Norfolk, and somewhere in Devonshire.

is not a large book in my edition.³³ I may be able to put it into your hands the first time I see you for I image you will not readily meet with it. Have you read any of D^r. Stennetts Sermons?³⁴ I hope when I write again to tell you more as perhaps our people here may examine into the State of affairs in the Church before them. How is Harvest with you? tis here on the whole good wheat especially & Fruit (apples &c) in very great abundance but of late [deleted] ^the^ Weather has been very uncertain & we have had much rain. Write again soon—please to give my respects to all Friends at B[ishop] B[urton] Hull &c. In the mean time May the Lord Bless you & preserve your going out & coming in from this time forth ever for evermore. I remain in duty & affections sincerely yours

Jo^s. Kinghorn

[p. 4]
The situation of the Country I will endeavor to attend to in my next as you see other subjects have this time precluded it & I apprehended you were less anxious about that than other things.

Rev^d. David Kinghorn
Bishop Burton
near Beverley
Yorkshire

[Stamp: August 21, 1788]

---

33 It refers to Richard Baxter's (1615–1691) *The Saints' Everlasting Rest; Or, a Treatise on the Blessed State of the Saints in Their Enjoyment of God in Heaven* (1650). According to Wilkin's catalogue, Joseph Kinghorn owned 31 titles written by Baxter. The copy of Baxter's *Saints Everlasting Rest* that Kinghorn owned was abridged by Benjamin Fawcett (1715–1780), which was published in Salop, Shropshire, in 1759. See [Wilkin, ed.,] *Catalogue*, 3-4. Joseph Kinghorn told his father in a previous letter, dated July 22, 1788, that he began to read Baxter's *Saints' Everlasting Rest*, abridged by Fawcett. Moreover, he believed that it "has not a single dry page in it. I think it one of the best practical books I ever read, and none of his peculiarities of sentiment appear in it, nor any of that severity and harshness that appears to have been so conspicuous in his controversial writings" (as quoted in Wilkin, *Joseph Kinghorn*, 126).

34 This could refer to either Joseph Stennett (1692–1758), who received an honorary Doctor of Divinity (D.D.) from the University of Edinburgh in 1754, or Samuel Stennett (1727–1795), the former's son, who received a D.D. from King's College, Aberdeen in 1763. Both were Seventh Day Baptists, who ministered to the congregation at Little Wild Street, London. Nevertheless, according to Wilkin's catalogue, Kinghorn did not own any of Joseph Stennett's works. Kinghorn owned the following works by Samuel Stennett: *Discourses on Personal Religion* (London, 1772); *Discourses on Domestic Duties* (London, 1783); *Remarks on the Christian Minister's Reasons for Administering Baptism by Sprinkling or Pouring of Water. In a Series of Letters to a Friend* (London, 1772); and *On the Parable of the Sower* (Edinburgh, 1801). See [Wilkin, ed.,] *Catalogue*, 41. Given the dates of publication, it is probable that Kinghorn was thinking about Samuel Stennett's *Discourses on Personal Religion*, and *Discourses on Domestic Duties*. Furthermore, when Kinghorn wrote to his father on June 25, 1788, he just came back from attending his friend James Hinton's ordination in Oxford, where he was introduced to Samuel Stennett (Wilkin, *Joseph Kinghorn*, 122).

Book reviews

Chun Tse, *The Marrow of Certainty: Thomas Boston's Theology of Assurance*, Reformed Historical Theology 77 (Göttingen: Vandenhoeck & Ruprecht, 2023), 302 pages.

The Marrow Controversy is well known in historical theology, especially among those who have an interest in the history of Reformed soteriology. Thomas Boston is a central figure in this controversy and his theology is the basis of Tse's thesis-turned-monograph, *The Marrow of Certainty*. Tse graduated with his doctorate in systematic theology from the University of Edinburgh and is currently an Assistant Professor of Biblical Studies (New Testament) at Carey Theological College, Vancouver, BC.

According to Tse, "This book aims to characterise for the first time the distinctive shape of Boston's overall theology and his doctrine of assurance" (20). Tse highlights the central importance of Boston's theology of union with Christ, and even says that union with Christ is "the controlling principle of his theology" and his lens for reading the *Marrow of Modern Divinity*. This helps to explain why the *Marrow* was interpreted differently between Boston and those who read it from a covenant theology perspective (121).

The method used by Tse in this monograph "is systematic in its organisation but historical in its methodology and analysis, striving to place Boston appropriately in his settings" (31). Following an introduction, the book is divided into five chapters. The first chapter situates Boston in his historical context, offering a biographical sketch detailing his life and influences. Chapter two compares the theology of Boston with the theology of the *Marrow*. Then, chapters three to five present a systematic presentation of Boston's theology: chapter three on "The Trinitarian, Covenantal, and Christological Dimensions of Assurance," chapter four on "The Soteriological Dimensions of Assurance," and chapter five on "The Ecclesiastical and Sacramental Dimensions of Assurance." Each chapter is further divided into subheadings to examine each theological loci.

This monograph is an excellent study of Boston's life and theology, and is a handbook of sorts for understanding Boston on his own terms and through his many writings. That being said, the focus on Boston's theology of assurance (especially in the systematic presentation of his thought) can be less overt at times. While Tse often directs the conversation back to Boston's theology of assurance, there are sections where he will expound on different aspects of Boston's theology only to then briefly connect the theme to his doctrine of assurance. Although connections to his view of assurance are regularly drawn out, they are not always raised as frequently or as explicitly as one may expect.

Yet although the work may be a bit broader in focus than what one might aniticipate, it nevertheless remains a very robust and helpful study of Boston's theology. It situates him historically, draws attention to the importance of his doctrine of union with Christ, expounds on his theology of assurance, and overall offers a resource for understanding Boston on his own terms.

Jonathan N. Cleland
PhD, Knox College
University of Toronto

Gudrun Andersson, and Jon Stobart, eds., *Daily Lives and Daily Routines in the Long Eighteenth Century* (New York: Routledge, 2022), 236 pages.

This recently published collection edited by Gudrun Andersson and Jon Stobart continues the pattern of the Routledge series that offers a wide variety of perspectives related to a certain theme. In this instance: domestic life in the long eighteenth century. Though broad here in the geographical sense (ranging from England to Japan), such snapshots of this period's domestic life are an invaluable addition to the historical inquiry in general, but of British (and British Baptist) history in particular. Each essay provides significant primary source interaction, drawing out microhistories to enhance the portrait of the century. The intention of the editors is established in their research question: "The study of everyday routines offers not simply an important window into the lives of a wide range of people but also a powerful analytical tool. The repeated nature of actions and their recurrence on a regular basis makes them critical in shaping identities, society, and space" (9).

True to form from the Routledge series, the primary sources are given priority in order to direct the scope of the investigation—namely, what may be discovered about variegated aspects of cultural sensibilities and their evolution (positively or negatively) as depicted in the primary source materials. They are even used to balance out one another, as one contributor notes these sources are scrutinized and cross-examined by contemporaneous works (e.g., the analyses of journals from visitors to Edo and the diaries of native women during the same period) (152). Summarizing the broader research question of the project, Andersson writes, "Daily routines bridged notions of private and public, local and national, domestic and commercial, past and present; indeed, they are the moment where all these intersect. Placing them in the foreground of our analyses is therefore vital to a fuller appreciation of the complexity of an individual's social milieu and to understanding how these aggregated into broader social practices and relations" (236).

This volume serves as a model for the utility of resourcing microhistories for their informational value alone. Quantitative, international snapshots of life in the period include a wide range from garden history to saké consumption—not necessarily for the purpose of building any specific case, but rather to retrieve historical data and identify life at ground level. The charts and graphs included in this collection offer remarkable appraisal of said data. Helen Brown and Jon Stobart demonstrate "how the everyday can be visualized and understood in aggregation as well as individually" for the Western communities represented in this moment (98–99). This aggregation is likewise furthered in Tara Hamling and Catherine Richardson's contribution, where they utilize account books and domestic purchase logs to index distinctions of lifestyle and class in the target period (21–22). Their analyses prove most fitting for showing the rhythm of the year, weekly or seasonal purchases, kinds of furniture, as well as housekeeping expenses. Along the way, they draw conclusions regarding the "shift in thinking from temporary to permanent domesticity" through the end of the century (31). The volume naturally transitions to an example of domestic life through the personal writing of a woman named Hannah, who may be considered a jackpot of microhistory *resourcement* in terms of the kinds of content she offers in her journals and correspondences. Thomas McGrath notices Hannah's cultural shift following her marriage and subsequent transition from rural to urban life. These materials reveal much of the social expectations of the household, especially as pertains to guests and hospitality in the urban environment and provide insight into the shift she experienced in her economic status (47). While it cannot be used to over-generalize, Hannah's account is one wherein she freely discussed her mental and emotional state, her frustrations with said domestic life, her acclimation and eventual comfort in her new status (57).

Continuing the theme of personal domestic content, Andersson uses a case study to explore some of the possible dynamics within marriages at the time. The diary of one Swedish man paints a picture of the expectations within his household during the period—the subject was in a tumultuous marriage and held an unpleasant attitude toward his wife and wrote about his depressive state (184). Bleak as such instances may be, Andersson reflects how such documents (alongside the writings of housekeeping notes and business records) reveal the social emphasis within the culture (170). These entries provide a stable control for the daily routines and family traditions of life in 18th century Sweden, while Johanna Ilmakunnas explains the other correspondences were intended to be read aloud around the "family or other circles" (65).

This volume does not remain only in theme of personal relationships and household sensibilities, however, and social activities and what may be considered "domestic necessities" receives attention as well. The occasioned permanent domesticity of the long eighteenth century, as abovementioned, reveals how the "horticulturalists and landowners became increasingly interested in their ability to control nature to increase productivity of their land" (88). Through numerous housekeeping collections, garden journals, and financial records of the period allow for the creation detailed graphs and charts to visualize garden history, both in the types of food grown the kinds of trees were cultivated and sought after by families. Although in terms of differences between the classes and landed peoples there is much left to discern concerning their garden culture.

While focused to the topic of domestic life and routines, the scope content is at times varied. Interestingly, the volume provides insight into night life—even the less savory activities—in Edo, Japan during the eighteenth century (and hypotheses related to the amount of saké produced and consumed). Included also is an essay on maritime life and sensibilities obtained from various ship logs and journals.

Readings through this collection of primary sources on the topic domestic life in this century provide for the reader a direct perspective into their minds and world. The sundry locations are not to suggest some kind of homogenous correlation (such as between a Swedish upper-class individual and an uneducated Baptist in lower-middle-class London), but exploration pertaining to specific locations might be of help in better understanding the microhistory of a particular region—and perhaps formulate a more standard pattern for cultural sensibilities. As more published works are developed in this series, those which depict British life will provide a more expansive aggregation of these sensibilities to those studying subject matter. This especially is to the great advantage of those connected with the readership of the *Journal of Andrew Fuller Studies*.

Christopher Ellis Osterbrock,
Puritan Reformed Theological Seminary
Senior Pastor, First Baptist Church of Wellsboro, PA

Matthew M. Reynolds, *The Spirituality of William Ward: Unsung Hero of the Serampore Mission* (West Lorne, ON: H&E, 2023), 274 pages.

Although William Carey (1761–1834) and his co-laborers in India have been an ongoing subject of interest for pioneering missionary efforts, relatively little has been written to explore the specific facets of their theology and spirituality. Whatever has been written of Carey on the matter, even less has been penned concerning the unsung heroes alongside Carey that made his missionary enterprise possible—namely, William Ward (1769–1823) and Joshua Marshman (1768–1837). In the *Spirituality of William Ward*, Matthew Reynolds makes a dent in both deficits. He examines Ward's theology and practice for its own sake while utilizing Ward as a unique window into the famous mission endeavors of the Baptist Missionary Society based in Serampore.

The book is parsed into five chapters. First, a robust account of Ward's biography is provided to contextualize the analysis of his life and thought. Reynolds showcases the breadth of Ward's contributions to the mission by exploring each of his many roles: printer, preacher, evangelist, mentor, mission administrator, missiologist, theologian, historian, draftsman, author, college professor, pastor, husband, father, counselor, peacemaker, and friend (33).

Chapter two locates Ward's theological foundations and determines the "essence" of Ward's spirituality. Ward's doctrinal underpinnings are on par with the band of Particular Baptist believers associated with Andrew Fuller (1754–1815), being an evangelical Calvinist himself. Reynolds thoroughly demonstrates Ward's commitments to the "five points" of Calvinistic doctrine in both his published and unpublished writings. Through this, a less predictable emphasis is uncovered by Reynolds: Ward's creed of love. Ward declared, "If I were asked for my creed, I could soon give it: God is love. ... *If God so loved us, we ought also to love one* another... Were I going to establish a church, I would have such a creed as this" (99). These two pillars, a robust evangelical Calvinism and a credal commitment to Christian love, permeated Ward's thought. What trickled down from his theology was a spirituality marked by prayer, humility, and usefulness. Reynolds argues that Ward consciously attempted to conform to his evaluation of the apostle Paul's theological and missiological ethos as he worked out his doctrine and practice (121).

Chapters three and four highlight the manifestation of Ward's spirituality in his personal and pastoral relationships, as well as in the working partnerships of the mission. The fruit of his spirituality made him a patient pastor, a peacemaker, and a mediating presence in times of controversy. Based on Ward's writings, it is clear he was shepherding more than Carey or Marshman. Reynolds documents Ward's consistent accounts of pastoring native converts in addition to Carey's sons, which point to a demeanor of patience in his discipling. Ward also served as the glue of the mission amongst the varying personalities involved in the endeavor, showing that Ward was respected as the reconciler of relationships.

Amongst other examples, Ward's peaceful mediation shines through in Reynolds documentation over disputes concerning the Lord's Supper and Serampore's printing strategy. The mission in India was not spared the infamous debate on open and closed communion among English Particular Baptists. Ward, an advocate of open communion, in own words, chose to "throw away the guns to preserve the ship" (224), essentially prioritizing unity by not pressing his convictions on his colleagues. As for the printing operation, Ward was initially skeptical of Carey and Marshman's ambitious scale and execution of production (209–10). He was no doubt the most qualified to scrutinize the enterprise as a professional printer, but he humbly deferred to his colleagues' vision and eventually turned optimistic to their strategy (214–6). Reynolds notes the counterfactual possibilities of the mission following Ward's initial wisdom, but nevertheless Ward was committed to peacemaking—a continuous fruit of his spirituality (215–6). The final chapter summarizes the end results of studying Ward's spirituality and takes stock of his legacy. Questions can be raised about Ward's commitment to unity as a tendency to resort to compromise, but in the end his preservative effect on the mission is worth honoring.

Reynolds' strengths include opting for what Christopher Smith has called a "trinitarian approach" to the Serampore Mission that honors Carey as a pioneer but emphasizes the contributions of Ward (and Marshman) that worked in harmony to bear fruit in India. Of course, Reynold's book is a needed addition to Ward studies in general, but it also provides a broader look into the pastoral ministry within the Serampore mission, an area of historical interest that is usually overshadowed by their printing enterprise. Another highlight is Reynolds documentation of Ward and the trio's deliberate attempt to understand and apply what they believed to be the methods of the apostle Paul, the Bible's "theologian and missionary par excellence" (54). Whether Ward and company succeeded or failed at that aspiration is the debate of missiologists, but Reynolds does the necessary job of a credible historian; he analyzed an emphasis that was paramount to the subjects under examination. More scholarly work needs to be commenced that explores this stated goal of the Serampore missionaries.

There is one theme that stood out as desperate for development within Ward studies after reading Reynolds' work. With Ward's hands-on approach to native converts, Reynolds highlights the Indian experiences of conversion, discipleship, and ministry at Serampore recorded by Ward. Reynolds makes an astute observation concerning how an Indian conversion illustrated by Ward was published in England with more dramatic language in its description of the depravity of Indians compared to milder account in his private journal (177n15). This instance illuminates a question that could use more attention considering the many descriptions of Indians and encounters with them. Did Ward have a defined theological and cultural anthropology? And how did it affect his view of Indians, particularly Hindus? Did he feel a need to present Indians to his countrymen in ways consistent with their assumptions about the natives they were sent to serve? An untapped text that needs to be examined is Ward's *A View of the History, Literature, and Mythology of the Hindoos: Including A Minute Description of Their Manners and Customs, and Translations from Their Principal Works in Two Volumes*. This work appeared in 1806 and went through multiple editions. Reynolds research stimulates questions like these that remain in need of development and excites those who are interested in studies of the Serampore mission beyond the biography of Carey.

Caleb Hawkins
PhD cand., The Southern Baptist Theological Seminary